"I feel tha words Dav .... in this book. I believe that Dave's humility and honesty of his past about the road God has taken him will deeply touch and open your heart. Dave is a man that walks with integrity and practices what he preaches. Now be warned that this book might not be for just anyone. If you are not serious about truly wanting to honor God with your purpose, then this book is not for you. If you are not looking to be challenged on your integrity and serving others, then this book is not for you either. However, if you are ready to embrace a road that will change you and your family, that will call you up and challenge you on the things the world just looks the other way on, then this book is definitely for you."

—Bill McGee, Men's Ministries Pastor,
Savannah Christian Church,
Savannah, Georgia, www.savmen.com

"Today finding a job, especially the "right" job, may be difficult. Government regulations have been unfavorable toward employers, and there have been other hindrances. However, the person who learns and exercises the principles that Dave Hilgendorf points out so accurately in this book can not only expect to find work, but enjoyable and rewarding work. That is simply because Dave has used principles gleaned from the Bible–the "Manufacturer's Handbook"–to construct a pathway to vocational prosperity. These principles are equally applicable to professionals, those who are responsible for our farms and homes, and to anyone who wishes for his life to glorify God and be beneficial to others. It will be time well spent for almost everyone."

—Marion Griffin, M.D.

"After reading the first few pages of Dave's book, I had the sense that he might have been watching me, or that I have said too much in conversation, but then realized that we have not spoken in some time. One cannot help but feel that "This book was written for me personally". It certainly has me thinking about how I approach my work and what I say about it to others. How I'm interacting with fellow workers and seeing them in a new light, but most importantly how I react towards God in my work. Not only has Dave's book got me thinking about it, but also how to apply it."

—Alf Basson
Director of Sales and Marketing
The Frog Switch and MFG. Co.

JESUS
IS AT WORK

DAVE HILGENDORF

JESUS
IS AT WORK

Having Joy and Purpose at Your Current Job

TATE PUBLISHING
AND ENTERPRISES, LLC

Published by Tate Publishing & Enterprises, LLC
127 E. Trade Center Terrace | Mustang, Oklahoma 73064 USA
1.888.361.9473 | www.tatepublishing.com

Tate Publishing is committed to excellence in the publishing industry. The company reflects the philosophy established by the founders, based on Psalm 68:11,
"The Lord gave the word and great was the company of those who published it."

Book design copyright © 2014 by Tate Publishing, LLC. All rights reserved.
Cover design by Nikolai Purpura
Interior design by Mary Jean Archival

Published in the United States of America

ISBN: 978-1-62994-451-7
Religion / Christian Life / Professional Growth
14.02.19

Acknowledgments

I want to thank Jesus Christ. With Him, my work has meaning.

I'd like to thank my wife, Kari. She's beautiful inside and out and truly a gift from God. Without her steadfast, reliable faith, her good judgment, her knowledge of Scripture, and her encouraging spirit, this book would not have been written.

I'd like to thank Andrew Wommack, for the huge impact his teaching has had on my understanding of God's unconditional grace, as well as all the other teachers and preachers in my life that have shared God's Word and increased my knowledge and understanding, most notably Pastor Cam Huxford and Pastors David and Deborah Garner.

I'd like to thank those whose advice helped me to get a book contract, including my friend John Crosby and the resources he recommended from Michael Hyatt.

I want to thank my parents for starting me off on the right path by faithfully taking me to church every Sunday and for always loving me unconditionally.

Contents

Foreword

What a spot for me to be in; I've never been a good reader—always been a writer; always had trouble sitting for long periods, concentrating on any one thing, etc., and now a good friend asks me to read his book and write the foreword!

Okay, so here I am, on vacation at Myrtle Beach, South Carolina, and I have actually read Dave's book entirely and thoroughly enjoyed it! At times, I felt as if my own thoughts were on the pages—funny how us Christian people think alike—but normally don't write our thoughts in one complete story as Dave has done here.

I realize only Dave could have written such a good, common-sensical, and timely book that has now challenged me to look at how I mix my faith with my work!

So many Scriptures to support his thoughts and points of view—you'll have no problem following his words of wisdom—and Dave takes us through our workday and asks us to consider how we are carrying ourselves; with Christ totally, with Christ partially, or with Christ like a pinch of salt or oregano!

Take it from a guy who has read a little over the years—this is a good read! But be careful: Dave reaches down and grabs God's principles of living and working and shares them with those of us willing to sit, relax, and take it in...then he asks us to act on it—this is where Dave is most interested for each of us: Can we act on what he has written to us?

Dave, thanks for putting yourself in this fine piece of work! It is awesome, and folks will receive a blessing...

Blessings to all,
Chuck Powers
Founder, Randolph Christian Men's Ministry

Introduction

G od has a much different view about the work people do than what most people have. Work is not a necessary evil, but rather a wonderful part of God's plan for mankind as well as for each and every person's life.

His plan for each person and, in particular, for the work they do was established before they were even born. The reason for their work is not just financial. In fact, the money they earn is probably the least of God's concern regarding their work.

People everywhere are searching for more than what they have. In response to what they think they're missing, they're blaming everyone and everything in their lives including their job, their boss, their coworkers, their spouses, and the balance in their bank accounts.

The good news is that to fill this God-sized hole in their hearts does not require that they make a major change in their circumstances.

They don't need to get a divorce.

They don't need to make more money.

They don't need that big promotion or a more impressive job title.

They don't need to quit their job in search of a better one.

They don't need to go back to school and get a degree, or another degree.

Their don't need to go into business for themselves so they can be their own boss and be more in control of the work they do and how they do it.

They don't need to devote their time and energy outside of work in a hobby or volunteer position that they think is more meaningful or more in line with their passion.

And they certainly don't need to grudgingly accept their lot in life and just wait it out until retirement before they start expecting more meaning and joy in their lives.

It sounds trite and so much like a pat Sunday school answer, but what they really need to fill that God-sized hole in their heart is Jesus. More to the point, what they really need is Jesus at their work.

Of course, Jesus is already at their work. He's not the problem. *They* are the problem.

They need to open their eyes and their hearts, renew their minds, and allow Jesus to work through them in a powerful way, in a way that only He can.

It's time for every believer to expect more out of their relationship with Jesus Christ than just a ticket to heaven when they die. He's not a fire insurance agent, as we so often treat Him. He has much greater plans for our lives here on this earth than we're settling for, and I believe our work is a big part of those plans He has for us. If we're smart, we should want more out of our work as well.

This book is about living out God's purpose and His assignment for us in our work, and the only way to do that is through His Son, Jesus Christ.

This book is not about finding the career in which God wants us to be, or pursuing a ministry or hobby we're passionate about, though we will address those issues during our journey together.

The good news is that even if the career choices you've made up to this point have not placed you in the specific job God intended for you to be in, I believe that like GPS, God recalculates based on our choices, "And we know that all things work together for good to those who love God, to those who are the called according to His purpose." Romans 8:28 (NKJV).

Once you realize you can live out your God-given purpose right where you are, you should start to look at your job, your career in a whole new way. You'll get a sense of just how important you are to God and how much He loves you and cares about the work you do. You'll see how much potential you have to be a positive force in the world all day, every day. Your deep longing to feel that what you do each day matters will begin to be satisfied.

Does it have to stop there? Do God's plans mean we have to stay doing just what we're currently doing for the rest of our lives? No, it doesn't have to *stop* there, but I believe it has to *start* there. We have to start seeing Jesus at work in our lives right where we are before we'll be ready for anything else.

This book is divided into four parts:

Part 1: Here's the Problem describes the nature and extent of the problem when people don't realize *Jesus is at Work*. They feel that something is missing in their work, a sense of divine purpose. Due to a lack of understanding, they try to compensate for this by making matters worse.

Part 2: Dream with Purpose shows how discontented workers can fix their problem God's way. They first need to understand the critical difference between God's *purpose* for their work and his *assignment*. Only after they have a divine purpose for their work can they discover God's assignment for their work. Throughout this process, they need to learn to let God be their promoter.

Part 3: Think Like Jesus shows how to take the next step by becoming a "living sacrifice" and becoming "transformed by the renewing of your mind" (See Romans 12:2, NKJV). By doing so, you'll learn and adopt God's view when it comes to work, money, full-time ministry, and retirement.

Part 4: Act Like Jesus looks at James 1:22 and challenges us to be doers and not just hearers of the Word. By getting yourselves, namely your flesh, out of the way and allowing Christ to work through you in your daily activities, you'll see amazing fruit. You'll be great at what you do. You'll be a model of integrity. You'll love and serve others, and you'll share the good news of the Gospel and make disciples.

I applaud you because by reading this book I assume you want more than the status quo when it comes to your work, more than just getting by, paying your dues, and paying your bills. You want to see and experience *Jesus at work* every day you step into your workplace so that you can have the joy and purpose through your work you've always desired.

You have an exciting journey ahead. You'll find that it's well worth the effort!

PART 1

Here's the Problem

"We have met the enemy and he is us[1]."

—Walt Kelly

First Things First

If you haven't received Jesus Christ as your Lord and Savior and been born again, I implore you to take care of this critical business with God. God's Word promises,

> [That] if you confess you confess with your mouth the Lord Jesus and believe in your heart that God has raised Him from the dead, you will be saved. For with the heart one believes unto righteousness, and with the mouth confession is made unto salvation... For "whoever calls on the name of the Lord shall be saved."
>
> Romans 10:9–10, 13 (NKJV)

Jesus said "Most assuredly, I say to you, unless one is born again, he cannot see the kingdom of God." (John 3:3 NKJV)

Although anyone can benefit from this book, it is written with the assumption that you, as the reader, are already saved, that you're born again.

This is not another self-help book that borrows truths from the Bible, repackages them, and then disseminates them under the pretence of being a new innovative idea.

This book is intended to share with you, a believer, some of what you may not already know about what the Bible already says about your work. As a result, hopefully you'll have a correct attitude about your work and your career.

I want to make sure you're saved before going forward because, for one thing I want you to be saved, but for another I believe we must be saved before we can be transformed by the renewing of our minds (see Romans 12:2 and 2 Corinthians 5:17).

My hope is that you'll renew your mind when it comes to the issue of your work and that in the process you'll appreciate all that God wants for you in this important aspect of your life. As a result, I pray that your career and your work will be filled with purpose, joy, satisfaction, and fulfillment in a way that can only come from a personal relationship with Jesus Christ.

There's no *magic prayer* that leads to salvation, but if you haven't been saved (or you're not sure if you have been), I believe you can change that by speaking a prayer like this and meaning it in your heart:

> Dear Lord Jesus,
>
> I know I am a sinner, and I ask for your forgiveness. I believe you died for my sins and rose from the dead. I trust and follow you as my Lord and Savior. Guide my life and help me to do your will.
>   In your name, amen.[2]

Apathy and Misery in the Workplace

Sam breathes a heavy sigh as he glances over his inventory report for the week.

The accounting department at headquarters will be expecting it by noon and he's a bit rushed to finish it up after a more-hectic-than-expected morning. He looks from the report up to the clock on the wall, then to the portrait on the right side of his cluttered desk showing the joy of his life, his wife, Jen, and three kids, Mary, Timothy, and Jeremy. He wishes he could muster up a smile to match those toothy grins looking back at him from the portrait, taken on a sunny day last year on their front porch.

"What's wrong with me?" Sam asks himself with silent desperation. He's asked that question for so long, and so many times, he can't remember when he started or how many times he's bounced it around his head.

Sam worked long hours and made sacrifices to get to his current position as manager of a prominent grocery store in a prosperous part of town.

His pay is better than average, he guesses. With his steady paycheck, he's been able to take care of his family's basic needs, plus some extras like the boat they bought last summer.

He enjoys his job, for the most part. He's respected by his employees and his peers, and he knows he's good at what he does. He gets frustrated at times with the lack of work ethic from some of the teenagers who report to him, but that's to be expected. On the plus side, he feels like he's helping them to mature and develop important job skills while they're earning money.

There's nothing inherently wrong with what he does. After all, the grocery store serves an important role in the community. He's always felt his company charged a fair price for a good product.

On top of that, everyone he works with thinks Sam has the perfect life and has it all together.

Why, then, does he feel so empty? He makes the twenty-three-minute drive to work every day feeling as though he's missing something but with no idea what he's missing. *There's got to be more to life than what I'm doing every day*, he thinks to himself.

On his way home each day, he wonders if what he does really matters. He feels like he's just treading water and adding up the days, but has no idea what to do to fix a career and life that seems more meaningless each day.

A Quiet Epidemic

Sam is not alone.

> "Surveys reveal that 65% of American workers
> are unhappy with their jobs. Many of them go to
> work simply because they have no other choice. "I
> owe, I owe, so it's off to work I go.""[3]

You may not be surprised by that statistic, particularly if you count yourself among the majority. The fact that the lack of a sense of purpose and meaning among workers is so common is truly sad. What may be even more tragic, though, is the sheer impact this has on the individual as well as the society at large.

When someone doesn't have a satisfactory answer to that age-old question "Why am I here?" they can get frustrated and depressed, which affects their own well-being as well as the well-being of everyone they interact with during the workday as well as outside of work.

When a mom or dad takes their work home with them, either physically or mentally, they're not available emotionally for their spouse and their kids. Their whole life becomes focused on their work, and they miss out on the other aspects of their lives. But what may be more common, and with a greater negative impact, is when mom or dad takes their *lack of purpose* for their work home with them. It's easier to leave your briefcase or tool bag at work than it is to forget about the sense of emptiness you've been feeling all day long.

Most of Our Lives

One reason the impact of a lack of purpose toward our work is so huge is simply because so much of our time is spent on the job.

It's been estimated that the average person will spend 91,250 hours in their lifetime working[4].

In theory, we spend half of our waking hours at our job. When you include commuting time and the time getting ready to leave in the morning as well as the time to wind down at home at night, we really spend most of our waking hours, or you could say most of our *lives*, working.

If we're trying to identify what aspect of our lives has the greatest potential to impact our sense of worth and purpose, we could argue that our work is the most important based simply on how much of our time is spent at our jobs.

Worse Than Misery

Though you may not feel depressed or even frustrated about your job, you may be experiencing something that is worse, and that is apathy. *Apathy* is defined as "absence or suppression of passion, emotion, or excitement. Lack of interest in or concern for things that others find moving or exciting."[5]

Can you relate to this definition, or do you recognize it in others with whom you work? Maybe you've said or heard spoken at your work the following phrases: "Another day, another dollar," "Another day, same old thing," "I'm just workin' for the weekend," "Thank God it's Friday," or, on Monday, "that weekend was too short." How about some of the bumper stickers you see, like, "I owe, I owe so off to work I go"? Talk like this is usually meant to be funny but I believe often reveals a very real attitude toward work.

Put on a Happy Face

What if you're not expressing thoughts and showing signs of apathy and misery at your workplace, and what if you don't see or hear much of that from others where you work? Does that mean everything is hunky-dory? Maybe, but maybe instead, you and others are just putting on a happy face.

Someone who lacks purpose in their work, in addition to feeling miserable and/or apathetic, may have the added frustration of thinking they're alone in their emptiness because everyone around them seems to have it all together. Particularly in America, where independence, self-confidence, and self-reliance are so highly valued, there's tremendous pressure to at least present the appearance that everything is great.

You've probably heard the phrase "big hat, no cattle." That usually refers to someone who puts on the appearance of having a lot of money but in reality not so much. I think that phrase applies equally well to someone who seems to be very confident, satisfied, and fulfilled, but in reality is desperate for meaning and purpose in their work and their lives.

Just like Sam, the grocery store manager who, to everyone he works with, seems to be self-assured and have it all together; but in reality he spends much of his time pondering on what is missing in his life and wondering how he can possibly fill that sense of emptiness.

If the problem is as big as what I've described, and I believe it is, what is the answer? What can the average worker do to obtain that elusive sense of purpose in their work? Unfortunately, all too often in their desperation they try to find a purpose in the wrong place and in the wrong way. In doing so, they unwittingly make their problem even worse.

We'll talk about that common mistake in the next chapter.

Out of the Frying Pan...

"Hello, earth to Kevin," Bob jokes as he waves his hand in front of his friend's face.

"Sorry, what did you say?" Kevin asks.

"Are you done with the sports section?" Bob asks for the second time.

"Sure, sorry about that."

Kevin smiles and hands Bob the newspaper across the break room table, glances at the clock on the wall, and takes another sip of his coffee. Kevin pauses to think not about the article on last weekend's football games but rather about his after-work activities for the week ahead:

Tonight he'll pick up his son Josh from soccer practice, hurry home, then drive to choir practice at church. Tomorrow morning, before work, he promised to meet Fred, the head usher at his church, to help fold the programs for next week's service. The pastor gave him a new believer follow-up card on Sunday, so he's got to find some time to give them a call, maybe at lunch today... no, today's no good; he'll have a short lunch with the unexpected transmission job on the Cadillac that came in this morning. Maybe tomorrow; better yet, he can call them on his drive home tonight; he'll see how it goes. Wednesday, of course, is church night. The evangelism committee he's on has its monthly meeting just before church this week. He'll have to remind his wife, Wendy. Hopefully she can drive the kids to church since he'll have to be there early. Thursday he said he'd help out at the soup kitchen over lunch. He's second guessing committing to that. There's really no way he can swing that one without taking a long lunch hour. His boss will probably understand, but what if they're really backed up with repair work that day?

A Great Beginning

Kevin's been a mechanic at Thompson Auto Repair on Felton Street for twelve years. He's arguably the best mechanic in the shop. He's always had a knack for cars and considers it a treat to be able to tear apart an engine and put it back together. He's not getting rich, but he does okay and is certainly thankful he has a good job when so many are without one these days.

A few years ago after he got a raise, he and Wendy decided he was making enough where she could quit her job as a hygienist and stay home to be a full-time mom for their two kids, Josh and Sarah. It wasn't long after that when his attitude started changing about his job. Before that, he drove to work every day thankful for his job. He enjoyed working on cars and was so glad to be able to provide for Wendy and the kids. After all, he did pretty well for someone without a college education.

He was born again in the middle of high school at a youth event at church. Not long after that, he met Wendy and they started dating. What a blessing she had been to him: beautiful, caring, kind, supportive. He couldn't ask for more in a wife, and together, they had brought two great kids into the world. They attended the same church he grew up in. His parents had moved out of state after their retirement, but he knew they loved the fact that he was an active member of Pine Hills Baptist Church. His mom and dad were married there and faithfully attended their whole lives right up until they decided to move to sunny Arizona just a few years ago. Of course, Kevin and Wendy married there as well, and it had been their church home together ever since.

The Comparison Game

Kevin's life seemed to be working so well, so why did he start feeling so negative about his work? He remembered a time when he would enjoy showing up at work every day, but then something changed.

Mondays seemed to be the worst. He used to really enjoy the pastor's sermon on Sunday and think about how to apply the message to his life. Instead, on Sunday and on into Monday, Kevin began to dwell on what a great work the pastor was doing for the Lord. He compared himself to the pastor and other staff members at the church. He wished he could say he was serving the Lord with his life but couldn't convince himself that was true.

He wanted his life to really matter in eternal terms. He thought about that moment in the afterlife where he would meet his Creator. He so much wanted to hear those words "well done good and faithful servant," but would he?

He didn't feel bad about his job in the sense that he was doing something wrong, but he wanted more than that. He genuinely loved the Lord and wanted to give Him his best. He wanted to be totally committed. But could he honestly do that as a mechanic? His answer to that question was always a no, or a maybe.

Out of the Frying Pan and into the Fire

He decided to do something about the situation. He wasn't prepared to quit his job and become a pastor and dreaded the notion of doing such a thing, but he could still get involved.

He started seeking out opportunities to volunteer at church and in the community. He soon found out there was no end to the number of ways he could serve. When word got out that he was an active volunteer, he noticed others started approaching him asking for him to get involved in their committee, event, or ministry. He felt guilty saying no, and very soon his already-busy schedule was filling up fast.

Now he had a new problem. He was overcommitted and burning the candle at both ends. It seemed there wasn't enough time in the day to keep up with all of his new obligations. While Wendy admired his willingness to help others, Kevin knew all these commitments were putting a strain on her and on their marriage. Wendy was picking up the slack at home when he wasn't available to help out because he was busy serving somewhere. He couldn't remember the last time he just sat down and played with his kids. Was this all worth it?

The worst part was he didn't feel any more fulfilled than before, only now he felt guilty about neglecting his wife and kids. With such a busy schedule and limited time, his job seemed more than ever to be an obstacle and not a blessing. How could he get all the things he felt he should be getting done in his personal life while spending so much of his day at his job?

Naturally, he wasn't getting enough sleep as a result of all this, which was why he was nodding off in the break room this morning and didn't hear his friend Bob asking for the newspaper. Kevin gets out of his chair and returns to the service bay where he has an oil change on a Ford Taurus waiting for him. He's confused, tired and frustrated, and he doesn't know what to do.

Buying into the Lie

Kevin is like many Christians who feel their job lives and their church lives are disconnected. They've bought into the lie that their job is just a job and has no spiritual relevance. As a result, they feel a self-imposed pressure to make up for the fact that they're not doing *God's work* when they go to their job every day.

Like a teakettle coming to temperature, at some point something has to give in to this pressure they place on themselves. A nonbeliever, facing similar pressure born out of stress, emptiness, and dissatisfaction with their lives and their work, might naturally turn to any manner of fleshly, carnal releases. The devil has an unending supply of tempting alternatives including alcohol, drugs, pornography, gambling, fornication, and marital affairs. Of course, he makes those temptations available to the

Christian as well, but I think that with a believer he focuses primarily on those activities that seem on the surface to be noble and God-pleasing.

Volunteering at church or another nonprofit organization by itself is a good thing and maybe is something God very much wants for you to pursue. But how do you know if that volunteer activity is a good thing or a distraction?

One warning sign is that if you're pursuing this new activity with the wrong attitude, out of guilt or obligation, or trying to compensate for something lacking in your work. Another danger sign would be if by committing to this new activity, you're making it difficult or impossible to stay true to a commitment you already have that you know is God's will, what you might call a nonnegotiable commitment. These nonnegotiable commitments might include a regular date night with your wife, helping out with the chores at home, attending an activity for your children, or spending regular quality time with your kids. And, in my opinion, this list of nonnegotiable commitments should also include having a good attitude toward your job.

You may not feel comfortable lumping together your job in the same category along with what you consider to be obviously God-pleasing activities like spending quality time with your wife and kids. If you feel that way, I'm glad you're reading this book. My hope and prayer is that by the time we're done going through this book together, your attitude toward your work will have changed. Hopefully by then, you'll have come to appreciate your work as something that is part of God's plan for your life, not an obstacle for that plan.

Hobby, Anyone?

There is another type of activity that can become a distraction and a snare for believer and nonbeliever alike. If taken to an extreme, the devil can use it to steal, kill, and destroy. I'm talking about a hobby.

Please don't stop reading! I'm not trying to take away your gardening, stamp collecting, hunting, or any other hobby or fun personal activity that's an important part of your life, provided it's used in a balanced way and with the right attitude.

Just as with the other activities we've been discussing, a hobby has the potential to be unhealthy and misguided if someone is trying to find purpose and fulfillment in their hobby as a result of having given up on finding that purpose in their work.

Am I saying it's wrong or unhealthy to find purpose and fulfillment in a hobby? No, but I do believe that sometimes both Christians and unbelievers devote themselves to hobbies and volunteer activities as a result of a misunderstanding of what the purpose is for their life, particularly for their work. In the process they may be cheating themselves out of everything God intended for their work.

You may be a bit confused at this point and wondering how to find that elusive purpose for your work to which I've been referring. We'll discuss that in the next chapter.

PART 2

Dream with Purpose

Delight yourself also in the Lord, And He shall
give you the desires of your heart.

—Psalm 37:4 (NKJV)

Start with Your Purpose

Hear, O Israel: The Lord our God, the Lord *is* one! You shall love the Lord your God with all your heart, with all your soul, and with all your strength.

—Deuteronomy 6:4-5 (NKJV)

In this is love, not that we loved God, but that He loved us and sent His Son *to be* the propitiation for our sins.

—1 John 4:10 (NKJV)

*B*eep, *beep*, *beep*, my alarm clock sounded off as my eyes popped open to see the ceiling above only visible from the night light in our bathroom nearby. I climbed out of bed and shuffled over to our dresser to stop the damage and let my wife get back to sleep.

Years ago I had read somewhere about the value of positioning my alarm clock out of reach, making me crawl out of bed to turn it off and hopefully in the process avoid the "snooze syndrome." I took that advice and for the most part, it had worked pretty well.

In my first-of-the-morning stupor, I had to remind myself what day it was. It was Saturday. That meant I didn't have to be up this early, but it was the second Saturday of the month when the Randolph Christian Men's Ministry got together for breakfast, fellowship, and a message tailored to men. I never regretted attending this event each month, and I knew it was worth more than the extra hour or so of sleep I would otherwise get before our three-year-old would provide her own "please get me chocolate milk" alarm clock.

As I drove through the small mountain that separated our home from the church where the group was meeting this month, I thought about which of my friends might be there this time, most of whom I only saw once a month at this event. My stomach growled as I pondered with anticipation the high-calorie southern-style feast of eggs, sausages, bacon, grits, biscuits, and gravy that were always a part of this gathering of guys.

I vaguely remembered from the reminder e-mail the week before the name of the speaker this month, a local bishop I had never heard of. I had no idea what message he was going to share. Just under an hour later, as Bishop Trogdon began his message, I scooped up the last bite of biscuit into my mouth and settled back in my chair.

I knew within two minutes that I was in for another God moment. The bishop was talking about something that had been weighing on me for some time. God had been giving me answers in bits and pieces from various sources, and I sensed that He was going to sum it all up for me this morning.

This new revelation would change my outlook toward my work and would alter in a major way the approach I would take toward the writing of this book.

Our Purpose is Different Than Our Assignment

The theme for the bishop's message was the difference between our purpose and our assignment, and I'm paraphrasing it here[6]:

> Our job, our career, our ministry are assignments from God. These are not to be confused with our purpose. Our purpose is the same for each and every one of us, and that is to be in love with and in fellowship with God. That's why God created Adam and that's why He created each and every one of us. God doesn't need our companionship and our love, but He desires it, so much so that He gave up His only Son so that our sin—the barrier keeping us from being in perfect fellowship with Him—could be forgiven and removed forever.

That wonderful purpose Bishop Trogdon spoke about—to know and love God—was the answer to the stirring in my heart and, I believe, the puzzle piece required to fill the hole in everyone's innermost being. This simple idea, loving God, is so complete and profound that it answers every question about why we're here and what our focus in life should be.

We don't have to *do*. We just have to *be*; be in love, that is, with our Creator. We are His bride, He's crazy about us, and we should be crazy about Him.

God's chosen people, the Jews, knew this life purpose long before Christ came to redeem us. Immediately after He gave them the law, Moses said, "Hear, O Israel: The LORD our God, the LORD *is* one! You shall love the LORD your God with all your heart, with all your soul, and with all your strength." (Deuteronomy 6:4-5 NKJV)

Jesus came to fulfill that law. One of the pharisees, a lawyer, asked Jesus what was the greatest commandment. Jesus responded by first quoting that passage in Deuteronomy, saying,

> 'You shall love the Lord your God with all your heart, with all your soul, and with all your mind.' This is *the* first and great commandment. And *the* second *is* like it: 'You shall love your neighbor as yourself.' On these two commandments hang all the Law and the Prophets.
>
> Matthew 22:37–40 (NKJV)

Jesus pointed us to our purpose, to love God, and implied that if we do that, we will naturally love each other.

Not only is our purpose different than our assignment, it's also more important than our assignment. Our purpose, to love and be in fellowship with God, is the most important part of our lives and our work. If we ever catch ourselves stressing over what our assignment is in life (what we do or accomplish each day), we can instantly receive peace from the knowledge that the most important thing to focus on is in fact our purpose and not our assignment. That purpose is very simple: love God.

Relationship vs. Legalism

At the heart of this difference between our work purpose and our work assignment is understanding that God wants a relationship with us more than He wants our productivity. God's will is going to be accomplished, with or without our participation (check out the book of Revelation, we know how everything is going to end).

That's not the point. He didn't go through the bother of creating the world and each and every one of us so He could have an army of worker bees doing His bidding. He created us so that He could have a relationship with us. That was the purpose of His act of creation as well as His plan of redemption through His Son Jesus Christ. And that is now our purpose—to love Him and have a relationship with Him. Any other purpose for our lives will be misguided and will fall far short of what it should be, or worse, will be in opposition to His will.

Have you ever heard that climbing a ladder is less important than first choosing the right ladder to climb?

The only thing, in my opinion, worse than having no purpose in life, is having the wrong purpose. A misguided, self-appointed purpose apart from God's purpose for us, though well meaning and lived out with passion, will result in selfish, empty, meaningless pursuits. It can also result in a spirit of legalism.

We all have a pretty good idea what it means to be legalistic but oftentimes don't recognize it in ourselves. We point fingers at the pharisees in the Bible as well as certain denominations or preachers in the body of Christ for being legalistic, but we don't see how *we* are putting faith in our works above our love for God.

One definition I've heard of legalism is when we have rules without relationship. I think of legalism as trying to earn God's favor by the good things we do and forgetting that we couldn't have any greater favor with God (or any less favor) than that which was provided by Jesus through His sacrifice and our acceptance of that free gift. When God sees you and me as believers, His children, He sees our spirits and He sees His perfect Son, Jesus. Nothing we can do or not do can change what He sees in us.

Our work assignment, therefore, is not and should not be a matter of us trying to please God, but rather our loving response to what God has done for us.

To do anything without that foundation of loving God is simply wasted effort. Paul expressed this powerfully in his letter to the church in Corinth:

> Though I speak with the tongues of men and of angels, but have not love, I have become sounding brass or a clanging cymbal. And though I have *the gift of* prophecy, and understand all mysteries and all knowledge, and though I have all faith, so that I could remove mountains, but have not love, I am nothing. And though I bestow all my goods to feed *the poor,* and though I give my body to be burned, but have not love, it profits me nothing.
>
> 1 Corinthians 13:1–3 (NKJV)

I don't know about you, but that passage really hits me hard. Take a moment and do the following exercise.

First, think about your job, where you go to work every day, and what you do during the day. Ponder on all the activities, accomplishments, or attitudes from your work experience up to this point that you are most proud of, or that you think were the most worthwhile, honorable, memorable, and pleasing to God. Please brainstorm for five minutes and fill in the blanks below.

_____

_____

_____

_____

_____

_____

_____

_____

_____

Next, pick the three items you listed above that you are the most proud of and that you think are the most worthwhile, and rewrite them on the lines below.

_____

_____

_____

Finally, take those three items and insert them into the following statement (in the appropriate verb or noun form) and then read it out loud to yourself.

Though I _____ but have not love, I have become sounding brass or a clanging cymbal. And though I have _____ but have not love, I am nothing. And though I _____ but have not love, it profits me nothing.

Does that help put things into perspective?

How Do I Live Out this Divine Purpose at My Work?

You may be asking, "How do I have a relationship with God, how do I love God while I'm at work, and what does that look like in real terms I can understand, relate to and put into practice?"

You may also be thinking, "My boss isn't paying me to read the Bible, spend long periods of time in quiet prayer, or break out in loud singing and worship, and if I did, I'd probably get fired and rightfully so."

These are fair questions and concerns. Here are some thoughts that may be helpful.

Meditate on His Word

Whether you are at home or at work, you can meditate on God's Word.

The best teaching I've heard about meditating on God's Word is from Andrew Wommack, which I will paraphrase here[7]:

> The Bible says to meditate on God's Word day and night (Joshua 1:8 and Psalm 1:2).
>
> This does not mean to literally be reading the Bible every moment of the day including when we would normally be sleeping. If it did, it would be impossible to be obedient to this command. Rather, it means to be so focused on God's Word that it stays on the forefront of our consciousness all the time.

Worrying is a form of meditation in the negative sense, whereas meditating on God's Word is meditation in the positive sense.

All of us can probably think of a time when we carried some of our personal baggage with us to work and kept that baggage all day even though we worked and put in our time just like any other day.

In the back of our mind, we may have had financial troubles, someone sick or dying in our family, or an argument with our spouse that was weighing on us mentally and emotionally.

We probably didn't think much of the fact that we spent time worrying while working, as long as it didn't interfere, at least too much, with our job performance.

Why not do the same thing, only in reverse? Meditating on God's Word can be as simple as focusing on a single verse we read before coming to work. In our mind's eye, we can picture what it means in our lives, or we can develop a mental picture of the circumstances surrounding the verse, either for the author when they wrote the verse or the events referred to in the verse.

I like to have some index cards with Bible verses in my car so I can review one or more before I leave my car and walk into work.

I also like to have scripture posted up in my cubicle so I can see it throughout the day.

Pray and Praise

Last I checked (for now anyway), we still live in a country that guarantees freedom of religion. There's no excuse for us not to pray to God and praise God anytime we want, including while we're at work.

"Rejoice in the Lord always. Again I will say, rejoice!" (Philippians 4:4 NKJV)

Note that Paul does not say "Rejoice in the Lord at church on Sunday," or "Rejoice in the Lord except when you're at work." He says *always* and by that I believe he means we should do so consistently and in every aspect of our lives, including and especially at work.

"Rejoice always, pray without ceasing, in everything give thanks; for this is the will of God in Christ Jesus for you" (1 Thessalonians 5:16-18 NKJV). That's one of my favorite verses and one I have right in front of me while I work all day.

My prayer life improved greatly when I made it less complicated and more personal.

I benefited a lot from a book I recommend by Andrew Wommack entitled "A Better Way to Pray"[8]

I try to consistently pray on my way to work, at my desk before I get started with my day, and when I eat at break time and lunch. I try to keep those prayers almost entirely focused on praise and thanksgiving.

Probably the most meaningful times spent in prayer, however, are not the routine events, but the unplanned, spontaneous times when I simply reach out, either in my mind or verbally, to God as I go through my day. When something good has happened, I thank Him. When I have a decision to make, I seek His guidance. When I'm nervous about a meeting I'm about to attend, I seek His peace. When someone says something that offends me or bothers me at work, I silently pray for the proper, loving response (which may be *no* response). The result for me is that I make better decisions and I have a reassurance that no matter what happens, I'm not alone. It also helps me keep my job and my work purpose in perspective.

Do I do this every day and as much as I want to or as much as I should? Absolutely not. There are some days when I look back and realize I've tried to do my work on my own without reaching out to God and loving Him at all. Those are usually the days that are the most frustrating and the ones for which I don't feel much purpose.

Wisdom and Peace

"Set your mind on things above, not on things on the earth." (Colossians 3:2 NKJV)

These words from Paul apply as well, or better, in the workplace as they do anyplace else.

When I'm eternally focused while I'm at work, I'm reminded that although the work I'm doing is important, its only real importance is the extent to which it fits into God's plan for my life. This brings me wisdom and it brings me peace.

"There is a way *that seems* right to a man, but its end *is* the way of death." (Proverbs 14:12 NKJV)

When we go about our workday doing things simply the way we think they should be done, we're headed for trouble. When we're seeking and loving God while we're at work, we have the wisdom and peace of God on our side.

We can love God and "set our mind on things above" while we are typing out an e-mail, talking with a coworker, hammering a nail, or any other activity that's a part of our daily work routine, all without it negatively affecting our effectiveness in our job. In fact, just the opposite is true. If we're loving God and focused on Him while we're at work, we'll have more joy and wisdom, we'll be a nicer person to work with, and we'll be more effective at what we do than ever before.

Just stop trying to do your job on your own and start seeking Him, and not just once in a while but all the time. You'll start to experience the divine purpose for your work you've always wanted.

It's Even Better than That!

At this point, I hope you agree with me how reassuring it is to know that when it comes to our life in general and our work specifically:

- God has already told us our purpose, we don't have to figure it out
- Our purpose is simple (love God)
- Our purpose is more important than our assignment

If that was the end of the story, that would be amazing and wonderful, but it's not the end of the story; it's even better than that!

Honestly, I never felt quite right about this chapter or this issue of my work purpose. I believed that what I had written was true and I thought my practical suggestions for loving God at work had helped me and would help others as well. Despite that, I still felt like it was too much like a checklist, an obligation. I felt like my advice could easily lead to more legalism and less relationship.

While this was on my mind, I heard a teaching that the original command to love God, which was part of the law given to Moses in Deuteronomy 6:4-5 and repeated by Jesus in Matthew 22:37, can only be fulfilled by us through grace.

Under grace, our only job is to simply receive by faith everything God has provided including, and most importantly, His love.

This is described so well in this verse: "In this is love, not that we loved God, but that He loved us and sent His Son *to be* the propitiation for our sins." (1 John 4:10 NKJV).

Is God good or what?

This blew me away and I believe was God speaking to me to make sure I included this important clarification before this book went to print.

The teacher went on to illustrate how our lives will change when we start focusing on *God's* love instead of on *our* love. He did this by comparing two of Jesus' disciples, Peter and John.

Peter was known for speaking boldly but not always backing up his words with his actions. When the disciples were gathered together for the last supper,

"Peter said to Him, "Lord, why can I not follow You now? I will lay down my life for Your sake." John 13:37 (NKJV).

By comparison, John was quietly resting in the love of Jesus.

"Now there was leaning on Jesus' bosom one of His disciples, whom Jesus loved" John 13:23 (NKJV).

Fast forward several hours and what results do you see from these disciples?

Peter ends up denying he knows Jesus three times, while John is the only disciple, as far as we know, that was at the foot of the cross when Jesus died.

I believe we can only have genuine love for God when our focus is on how much He loves us. When we're conscious of how intense and perfect His love is, then and only then will we respond to Him and others with the love that He asks from us.

Keep It Simple, Labor Into His Rest, and Be Passionate

As we go on in this book to talk about God's assignment for your work and the beliefs, attitudes, and actions that you will naturally have as a result of your purpose, please remember this chapter.

Don't forget the difference between our purpose and our assignment; and when it comes to our purpose, remember to keep it simple, rest in and celebrate the finished work of Jesus, and be passionate about what He has done for you. The most important thing to be focused on, and the purpose of our life and our work, is to love God, and the best way to do that is to simply receive His love!

David described the passionate love he had for his Creator so well. "As the deer pants for the water brooks, So pants my soul for You, O God." (Psalm 42:1 NKJV).

As we go to work each day and throughout our work day, may we share David's passion and desire to connect with, reach out to, and love God.

Take a deep breath and meditate for a moment on this important truth that God has a purpose for you and your work, and that is for you to love Him. He loves you more than you could ever imagine, and now you can stop worrying about the purpose of your work. It's simply to return to Him the love He's already freely given and expressed to you. Having our work purpose firmly in mind, let's dig into what God's assignment is for your work.

Next, Find Your Assignment

The bell rang marking the end of third period and my English class. I had a free hour coming up and so I decided to check out the Career Day activities going on in the gym that day.

I was a junior at my high school; and although I was a hardworking student with good grades, I was a little frustrated about not knowing exactly what I was going to do after graduation. My older brother Steve had surprised the family a bit when he joined the navy. I figured he for sure would be going to college right away. After enlisting, he entered their officer training program and would ultimately attend the Naval Academy. Primarily because of my familiarity with my brother's experience up to that point and his enthusiasm about the choice he had made, I decided to stop and talk with a recruiter at the table set up for the navy.

After discussing that I was probably interested in going to college, he told me about the ROTC (Reserve Officer Training Corps) program the navy had. Basically, if I were accepted into the program, the navy would pay for me to attend college. In exchange, I would participate in ROTC activities while I was in college and then would immediately enter into service after college for a certain number of years. I hadn't seriously considered the military up to that point, but it sounded pretty intriguing. It would address concerns I had about paying for college and at the same time give me some direction that I was lacking up to that point.

The recruiter sensed enough interest on my part to ask me if I wanted to take an aptitude test to get an idea if I was a good fit for the program. That surprised me a bit. I hadn't dealt much with salesmen in my life up to that point, and I hadn't thought that my expression of interest in this case might lead to immediate action. Nevertheless, I agreed to his suggestion. I had enough time before my next class to take the test. I wasn't particularly interested in checking out the rest of the tables, and after all, I wasn't committing my life just yet; it was just a first step in the process.

The young man in the shiny blue uniform led me to a table set up between his recruiting display and the folded-up bleachers. After I was seated, he went to grab some paperwork. He returned with an envelope and a pencil.

"Answer each question with your first response and answer every question," he said. "I'll be back to check on you in a little while."

I had taken aptitude tests before. I couldn't recall what careers they had pointed me to, but I remember wondering what considerations were given to developing each of the questions on those tests. I knew in this case that the purpose was not to find out my ideal career, it was to find out if I was a good fit for a specific career, a *navy* career.

Midway through the first page, I read, "I would rather do the following: A. Play tennis B. Play football."

Interesting. What were they looking for here? Tennis was more of an individual sport and not very physical. Football, just the opposite—a team sport where getting beat up and bruised was part of the package. Surely they were looking for football players over tennis players. This was a problem. I loved tennis, and though I had always enjoyed tossing the Nerf football with a neighborhood friend or two growing up, my experience playing football as a team sport had been less than stellar.

I thought back to seventh grade to the one and only time I tried out for the football team. I made the team, but, as I recall, pretty much everyone did. It was cool to be able to put on the shoulder pads and the uniform; not so cool that my main job became running in the plays. I don't think I handled the ball once that year.

"You're still on the first page?" the recruiter asked with disappointment as he returned to check in on me and interrupt my mental stroll down junior high lane. "You're not supposed to analyze these questions. Now hurry up and answer them with your first response."

Woah, this wasn't the smiling, encouraging man I met on the other side of that display a half hour ago. I thought about the movie *An Officer and a Gentleman*[9] that came out a few years earlier. The drill sergeant, Emil Foley, played by Louis Gossett, Jr., gave the third degree to the new officer recruits, including the main character Zack Mayo played by Richard Gere.

I felt a little bit like Zack as I returned to my paper and pencil and dutifully hurried through the remainder of the test. I don't remember if I selected tennis or football on that question, but I never did become a sailor.

Finding Your Assignment— The World's Way

That aptitude test and others I've taken illustrate well how the world tries to determine the type of work or career for which each of us are best suited. Many books have been written about how to find the perfect job, the one occupation that fits you like a glove, the one you were made for, the dream job, what I would call your divine assignment.

From what I've seen, these books and conventional wisdom in general tend to ask you to focus on one or more of the following four factors when searching for the perfect job.

Your personality

The question about my preference for playing tennis versus football, along with many others on my ROTC test, was primarily attempting to find out about my personality. Another word for our personality is our soul, or more specifically our mind, will, and emotions. A combination of our genetic makeup as well as our environment, our personality encompasses what we think and how we react in response to various stimuli or circumstances in our lives.

The presumption when focusing on our personality in our job search is that we can't fight who we are and so we should embrace it and seek a job that seems to fit us best.

Your strengths

Another popular approach to discovering the perfect job is to focus on your strengths—those talents and abilities which come most naturally for you.

We're all different, and for a variety of reasons some of us are better at certain tasks and skills than are others. If we all identified and devoted our time and energies to what it is we're most effective, so the theory goes, we would all be more accomplished and happier. Just as with the case for considering our personality, I understand the logic behind this approach from a worldly perspective. I wonder, though, if these are the right things to consider if we're trying to discern what God's will is for our work.

The extent to which we have a predisposition toward a certain personality or ability, you could argue (and many authors have made this argument) that God created us a certain way because He wanted us to take advantage of those items in our plus column. In other words, you could say that He equipped us with our strengths and our personalities both to provide the tools to accomplish His desired result and to give us an indicator or guide to communicate to us which direction He wanted us to go with our time, efforts, and work.

You *could* make that argument, but before we settle on this and select an action plan, let's look at the next two factors.

Your desires

Another consideration often recommended by conventional wisdom—by the world—is to look inside ourselves and ask ourselves what our desires are. What excites us, motivates and energizes us? What would we do even if we weren't getting paid?

This factor is looked to as an important indicator by both Christians and non–Christians.

In his book *The Power of a Dream*[10], Bill Godwin encourages the reader to focus on their passion as the power that fuels their dream that God has for their lives. In his book *Quitter*[11], Jon Acuff suggests that figuring out your perfect job is more about recalling what you've already enjoyed doing in the past than it is about figuring out what you want to do.

By the way, those are both great books. Bill Godwin's book, in particular, helped me develop a plan that eventually led to me writing this book.

Your experience

Still another guide we are often asked to follow when analyzing what work we should pursue is what experience we already have. The argument is that our experience and the resulting knowledge and skills we have developed are assets that can be used to make us more effective with certain jobs than with others.

You need only look at sample resumes to see how much importance is typically placed on this factor. In fact, from what I've seen, experience is the primary consideration in the hiring process. All other things being equal, the logic goes, a hiring manager can assume that someone with more relevant experience than the next candidate will get up to speed more quickly in their work and in the process save the hiring employer time and money. The fact that the job candidate already has the desired experience may also be an indication that they previously satisfied the other factors we've mentioned (personality, strengths, and desire). In a way, then, the experience factor can arguably encompass all the key factors.

Remember God

Thoughts from this next section relied heavily on teaching from Andrew Wommack, specifically "Spirit, Soul and Body"[12] and "How to Follow God's Will,"[13]

I can understand why in the world hiring managers and navy recruiters would place so much emphasis on these four factors in selecting their ideal candidates. I can also understand why anyone who is relying on conventional, worldly wisdom to find their perfect job would likewise lean heavily on these four factors. But should we, as believers who are seeking God's will for the type of career we're to pursue, consider these factors as well and with the same level of importance?

My quick answer is "Yes, if…God."

Let's relook at the four factors just mentioned and discuss the best way to think of them from a biblical perspective. First let's look at our personality.

Our personality is only one part of who we are. We also have a body and we have a spirit. I believe that as a born-again believer, our spirit is what defines us. We *are* a spirit, we *have* a soul, and we *live in* a body. Our born-again spirit is perfect in Christ, and when we die our spirit will be joined with our soul and body in a way I don't fully understand but believe to be true, because the Bible says it's true (see 1 Thessalonians 5:23, John 3:6, John 6:63, Romans 8:22–23, 1 Thessalonians 4:17 for starters).

If we misunderstand our true identity, which is defined by our spirit, then we can make the mistake of focusing too much attention on our personality (our soul) or our physical traits (our body).

When considering how much to focus on our strengths, we should remember that God sometimes works through our weaknesses as much as, or even more than, through our strengths.

"But God has chosen the foolish things of the world to put to shame the wise, and God has chosen the weak things of the world to put to shame the things which are mighty." (1 Corinthians 1:27 NKJV)

With regard to experience, we may view our past experience as an incredible asset, but the reality is that God may have never intended us to gain that experience in the first place. The fact that we have a certain level of experience may be the result of choices we made that were counter to God's best plan for us. In addition, God may want us to succeed in an area we're not experienced in simply so that there will be no doubt in our mind, or in the minds of others in our lives, that the success came from Him and not from us.

Does He do that because He has a big ego and just wants the credit? Well, if He did want the credit, He has every right to demand and expect it. I think a more accurate way of understanding this, though, is that God wants to draw all men and women to Him; and if our successes only point others to us and not to Him, then we missed the big picture entirely.

How about our desires? To better understand how our desires should be an indicator of God's ultimate plan for our work, I think you have to start with a proper understanding of this passage: "Trust in the LORD, and do good; Dwell in the land, and feed on His faithfulness. Delight yourself also in the LORD, And He shall give you the desires of your heart. Commit your way to the LORD, Trust also in Him, And He shall bring *it* to pass." (Psalm 37:3-5 NKJV)

A number of God's promises in the Bible are unconditional, but this is not one of them. In order to receive the desires of your heart, you must do several things, according to these verses. First, you must trust in the Lord and do good. Next, you must dwell in the land and feed on His faithfulness. Finally, you must delight yourself in the Lord, commit your way to Him, and trust in Him.

If a Christian believes that God is going to give them what they want, independent of what their desire is or independent of what kind of relationship they have with their Creator, they haven't read these verses very closely. To me, these verses describe someone who is passionately and consistently devoted to, in love with, and obedient unto their Lord. They describe a state of being toward which I am striving but certainly have not attained. As one of my favorite teachers Andrew Wommack likes to say, "I haven't arrived but I've left."

I believe the degree to which God gives me what I want is dependent on the degree to which my life looks like these verses. Why? Because if God is truly number one in my life, if I'm seeking Him and desiring His will above mine, then my desires will naturally be aligned with His desires. Another way of saying this is that my desires will come from His desires. To me, this just makes sense.

Why would God want us to pursue our own desires or for that matter grant us our desires if they're inconsistent with His desires? He is God after all. He's all-knowing and therefore, by definition, He knows what's best for us. That's true for broader, general issues of right and wrong as well as very specific questions of whom we should marry, what job we should pursue, and what car we should buy.

If He really loves us, which He does (more than we can imagine), and He knows what's best for us, it makes sense to me at least that He would want our desires to match His desires.

Don't Do This at Home

Here's how I used to think about my dreams. I share this as an illustration of how *not* to use your desires when it comes to making plans for your work and career. I used to think that the real meaning of life, what made life worth living, was to pursue and achieve my dream or dreams. I typically was not sure what those dreams were. If I thought I did know what they were, they were usually borrowed from someone else's dream, or at least were strongly influenced by someone or something out there in the world. Inevitably, either I didn't achieve my dream (and felt like a failure) or I did achieve my dream and felt let-down or dissatisfied with the end result. In either case, I would then change my dream to something different, and on and on it went.

Despite the inconsistency, uncertainty, and disappointment of my dreams, the importance I placed on them was nothing less than being the key (so I thought) to my life purpose. At the same time, I viewed God and His will as being apart from and in competition with my dreams. As a result, I compartmentalized God. I didn't reject Him outright, that would have been foolish (I thought). I mean, He was God after all, and He did have the keys to eternal life in His hands.

But I figured I knew best what my dreams were and should be, and so I tried not to let my religion have too much influence on my everyday life. There was too great of a risk, in my mind, that God's will might start to steal my dreams and my happiness away from me.

In my old way of thinking, I didn't know God's will for my life, and frankly I really didn't want to know it. The people whom I thought had submitted to God's will (in my mind primarily pastors and missionaries) looked like they had signed up for a life of sacrifice, poverty, and not much fun. They may have taken comfort knowing they were pleasing God with their occupation and the way they spent their time, I thought, but they sure were missing out.

And after all, my thought process continued, I was saved by grace, and so all of us believers were going to end up in heaven anyway, so why not have fun and pursue *my* dreams while I'm here, but keep God enough in my life to maintain my "Get Out of Earth and Stay Out of Hell" free card?

That all sounds pretty silly when I think about it now, but it didn't back then. It was serious business given that my happiness hung in the balance, or so I thought. In reality, my happiness, and much more than my happiness, did actually hang in the balance. What I *didn't* realize was that not only was God *not* in competition with my happiness, joy and purpose, He was the only chance I had of ever attaining those things. There's much more to that story, but to sum it up, I became born again; and by renewing my mind through God's Word, I learned that eternal life was about much more than going to heaven. Jesus said, "And this is eternal life, that they may know You, the only true God, and Jesus Christ whom You have sent." (John 17:3 NKJV)

A Step-by-Step Plan (kind of) for Finding and Knowing Your Divine Work Assignment

If you were hoping to find out what career you should pursue after reading this book, or in particular, this chapter, at this point you may be a little disappointed. You may, in fact, be doubly frustrated in sensing that I've asked you not to rely too heavily on the tools you were primarily planning on using to figure this out. If you're like me, you want someone to give you a step-by-step plan, a checklist or blueprint to follow that will help you get to your goal quickly and easily.

If that describes you, then read on. Although I don't believe that shortcuts are God's way of doing things, I do think there's a proper order of doing things, so I thought I'd gather my thoughts on this issue into a list of action items.

Whether you're a teenager or in your fifties or older and you want to seek out, know, and live out God's specific will for your work and career, you may benefit from following these steps:

1. Remember what we discussed in chapter 4—that the purpose of your work is to love God. Try not to forget that, and don't confuse your purpose with your assignment. Read Matthew 22:37–40 and 1 Corinthians 13:1–3.

2. Believe that God cares about the details in your life and has a perfect job in mind for you. He has an opinion about your career, and it's better than your opinion. Read Luke 12:7 and Isaiah 55:9.

3. Develop an attitude of gratitude for your current work situation, whatever it is, including a lack of a job if that is the case. Read Philippians 4:4 and 1 Thessalonians 5:16–18.

4. Seek and cultivate a relationship with God; and while you're doing so, seek a revelation from Him through His Word and through prayer exactly what job He wants you to have. Place a lower priority on your personality, strengths, and experience, and a higher priority on God's will and desire for you. Consider your own desires for a career only if you're truly seeking and loving God. If you're doing that, His Word says that He will place His desires for a job into your heart and make them your desires. Read Philippians 4:6 and Psalm 37:3–5.

5. If you're certain you've received a revelation of God's will for your career and it happens to be different than your current career or work situation, pursue with passion and diligence a change in your current job, but seek God's will on the wisest way to do this.

6. If you're not sure of God's will for your career, then focus on, appreciate, and be faithful to what God has already given to you. Don't stress over your uncertainty, continue to seek clarity on the issue; and while you're doing that, learn and apply some of the ideas discussed later in the book about acting like Jesus at your work.

You may find yourself having trouble following these steps and instead wanting to shortcut the process and just do what *you* think is best. Don't do it! That's called self-promotion; it's foolish, and you'll regret it.

Avoiding that mistake is the focus of our next chapter.

Let God Be Your Promoter

I can't wait to see what God has in store for us next!

—Kari, my wife, June 2009

If you're considering quitting your job in order to promote yourself, pursue your dreams, make more money, take on more responsibility, or have a greater sense of purpose and meaning in your work, I'd like to ask you to read on, pray on, and take to heart what God has placed on my heart on this matter.

Indulge me, if you will, for a few moments while I share part of my story and how God has used it to shape my view of my work as well as the concepts of self-help and self-promotion.

In the mid '90s, I found myself with what most people would consider a great job with a good income as an engineer for a large, prosperous company. Unfortunately, I was not happy. Why? At the time, I thought the reason for my unhappiness was that my job was not satisfying my innermost desires.

I was a churchgoer at that time, just as I had been all of my life, but I was not born again. I had not yet accepted

Christ as my personal Lord and Savior. I had a lot of priorities in my life that mostly focused on satisfying my own selfish needs and desires.

I know that God was not my number one priority. My marriage wasn't either. I suppose if I had to name the highest priority in my life at that time, it would have been my job. Because of that, I began to blame that job for a lack of satisfaction in my life. If I had known back then that I had a God-sized hole in my heart that could only be filled by Him, I would have had a completely different outlook on my marriage, my job, and everything else in my life.

Unfortunately, I didn't realize that truth and I started to seek purpose through an adventure. My adventure of choice was to quit my job and start my own business. This didn't happen overnight. It started when after working full-time for a while, I was intrigued by a late night infomercial that talked about becoming financially independent buying and selling real estate. This, I thought, might be the ticket to finding something more.

After buying that course and trying out a few of its suggestions and then moving to a new area where real estate investing was very popular, I decided to attend a seminar on the topic. From that event I learned about and later attended a different, bigger real estate seminar.

At that second event, the self-anointed guru talked about how easy it was to get rich quickly in real estate and how all of our jobs were holding us back from the financial freedom and independence we had always wanted.

"Do you know what your job stands for?" the guru asked rhetorically. "Just over broke, and that's what you'll be as long as you stay where you're at!"

I was mesmerized by this speaker. My appetite for a life purpose was wetted. A fire had been lit under my fleshly desire, or lust, for money and the world's version of freedom as it had never been before.

I started to attend other seminars and to purchase home study courses and books on real estate and getting rich. If someone seemed to have the supposed magic pill and shortcut to financial independence, then I was interested, and I was willing to spend pretty much whatever time or money was necessary to obtain it.

Once I actually took action and started to make some money in real estate, it was just a matter of time before I felt I needed to quit my job and run my new business full-time. The fact that I wasn't in any position financially to do so didn't seem to matter. I took off on my own in January 2000.

To make a long story short, I never did find the purpose or happiness I sought through that business. After neglecting my marriage and getting a divorce, I continued to pursue my business with intensity. Mainly out of pride, I was determined not to fail. I worked tirelessly. I bought, sold, and rented hundreds of homes.

Like an addict grabbing another needle for an already mutilated arm, when I didn't get the money, success, freedom, or sense of purpose I had sought, I continued to do more and more deals. I used debt to keep my business afloat, but it was a house of cards. When the financial and housing markets crashed in 2008, my business had already been dead for a while.

I filed bankruptcy for over a million dollars of debt.

The good news is that at some point in this story, in the midst of my brokenness, I started attending a new church. I met my future wife, Kari, and her two wonderful daughters; and on Father's Day, 2005, I committed myself to Jesus Christ and was born again.

From that point forward, I began to renew my mind through God's Word for every area of my life, including my work and my career.

I started to realize that my job was never the problem. *I* was the problem.

I started to realize that finding and having a purpose as well as freedom—real freedom—had nothing to do with the worldly things that had consumed my energy and my time up to that point. It had to do with a relationship with my Creator. Through that relationship, God would begin to show me a better path, a path based on His plans for my life and for my work.

Never again would I have to struggle with the sense of emptiness in my work that I once had felt.

Don't Promote Yourself, Leave That to God

Bolstered with these powerful truths, I returned with a positive attitude to the work force as an engineer after being self-employed for eight years, thanks in part to a referral from a friend I met through the men's ministry at my church. There were a lot of great things about my new job. I was able to define my work hours and actually have a personal life outside of work, something I never had with my business. I was able to focus on the things I did best rather than wear twenty different hats. I had a predictable income, making it so much easier to have a budget and work on the financial plan my wife and I had learned from Dave Ramsey's Financial Peace University[14]

There were also a number of things about my new job I didn't like. Most of my coworkers used foul language and gossiped, something that wouldn't have bothered me much in the past but now really annoyed me. Although I enjoyed many aspects of having a boss again, especially the part about not being responsible for everything going on in the business, I was frustrated by the micromanagement style of my new boss. This time around, though, I was determined not to let my perceived negatives of my job steal my joy nor take away from me this new sense of purpose I had for my life and for my work.

I ruled out the possibility of taking matters into my own hands by quitting a job that seemed less than ideal. I stayed faithful to the job and to my obligations at work. After being employed for a year at that job, I was told my job was being eliminated due to budget cuts, and I was let go.

I'll never forget that day. I was called by my boss to meet him in the company library. I knew something was up because he had never done that before. He had one of the workers at his side, I guess in case things didn't go smoothly and to walk me out of the property in an orderly fashion.

He told me that I wasn't being let go for any performance issues, but rather they had run out of capital money for projects, the management of which was my reason for being there.

Within one hour from when I walked in that room, I had cleaned out my desk, said my good-byes to fellow coworkers, and driven out of the parking lot for the last time. I had previously arranged to meet for lunch with a friend, a fellow believer from my church. I went straight to meet with him and share what had just happened. Amazingly, I wasn't stressed as I told him. Similarly, he didn't respond with anxiety or concern. I then stepped outside of the restaurant to call my wife, Kari, and tell her the news.

Her first reaction was laughter. "I can't wait to see what God has in store for us next!" she said.

What a blessing it was to face the giants of uncertainty that were ahead of me with such a sense of peace—peace from within and peace from the believers in my life, all of which was divine peace from my Father, peace that transcends all understanding (see Philippians 4:7). That would never have been possible without a relationship with God.

To make another long story short, in less than two months in a recession economy, God provided me and my family a better job, working for a better company in a better location, in a better working environment, with a better boss, and with better pay.

If I ever have the pleasure of sitting down with you over some coffee, I would love to share with you some of the countless creative and surprising ways God has been blessing our socks off ever since, and continues to do so every day.

Is It Ever Okay to Quit?

Am I saying you should never quit your job?

No, that's not what I am saying. I realize that some of you reading this right now are in jobs you should not be in, and God's will is for you to quit, maybe even tomorrow.

As we discussed in step 5 of the action plan at the end of the last chapter, if you're pursuing God and making

him number one in your life, and you're confident that
He's revealed to you that you should pursue another job
or career, go for it! Remember, when I made the mistake
of quitting my job, I was certainly not making God my
number one priority, and I don't believe my desires were
the same as His desires.

Without knowing your exact situation, though, in
general, I am asking you not to rush into a decision to quit
your job in a similar way I would advise another believer
who is unhappy in their marriage not to rush into a
divorce. I realize these situations are not equivalent since
the Bible offers very specific advice regarding divorce, but
it gives you a sense of how strong I feel about this issue.

Oftentimes, changing our circumstances seems like a
quick escape, a quick fix, to what we perceive to be what's
wrong with our lives, when in fact God might want us to
stay right where we are.

Why would He want us to stay in a situation that
doesn't feel right to us? I won't pretend to know the answer
to that question, but here are some possible answers.

- He may want you to grow and mature after going
  through some struggles.
- He may want you to be impacted by someone or
  something that you would otherwise miss.
- He may want someone else to be impacted by *you*.
- He may want to promote you in a supernatural
  way, in a way that you and others will know could
  only have come from Him. This may be to grow
  your faith or to provide you with a testimony you
  can give to others.

Be Content and Trust Him with the Big Picture

The degree to which you are content, thankful, seeking God's will, and trusting God to promote you will have a big impact on how you view your present work situation. It will also have a big impact on how you view your future. In particular, it will play a large part in whether you find peace and joy in your work and career now or whether you put off that peace and joy to an unknown future, to a future job or to your future retirement.

I don't know specifically what God's will is for the type of work you do or should be doing. In fact, to be perfectly honest, I don't know with certainty that I'm in the *exact* job God wants for *me*. Am I satisfied with that uncertainty? No, I'm not. Am I happy and at peace with God while living with some uncertainty about the work I do? Yes, I am.

One reason I'm at peace is that I'm trusting God with the big picture while at the same time seeking His guidance with the smaller picture, primarily through His Word and through prayer. It may be that the adventure that God wants for you in the job you're currently at is much better than anything you could achieve through starting and running a successful business, going back to school, finding a different job, or whatever other change you're feeling drawn to make in your work life. Or it may be that God does want you to quit your job...but not yet.

How will you know what to do? Don't try to figure it all out at once, but rather take it step by step.

"Your word is a lamp to my feet and a light to my path." (Psalm 119:105 NKJV)

Think of yourself walking down the path of your job and your career. As you seek God through His Word and through prayer, He will provide enough light for you to see your feet and the path just ahead, but probably not more than that. Rather than jumping off your path or standing stuck in one place in your path, try allowing God's Word to direct you to the next few feet of your path.

God might be helping you grow spiritually, financially, and emotionally through small moves while at the same time preparing you for the big move (and the blessings that will come with it) that He has in mind for you later down your path.

While at your current job, be still (Psalm 46:10), be obedient, and seek His face (relationship) more so than His hands (what He can give you). You might find the purpose, joy, and peace you're looking for in your work without going through the heartache and pain that I went through when I quit my job…and you might be able to do so right where you are right now.

Or you may have to be patient and let God prepare you for what He has in mind for you later, in His time.

Joseph as a Role Model

It may be helpful and inspiring for you to read or reread the story of Joseph found at the end of the book of Genesis.

In the same way you may feel frustrated with the job you're in right now, Joseph ended up in many situations through his experiences that most likely did not appear to be God's will or to have any benefit or value. Joseph remained patient and faithful through all of these trials, though, and in the end he realized and proclaimed to his brothers that God had sent him to Egypt for a greater purpose—to save his family as well as all the people of Egypt from the great famine.

I'm sure he didn't realize how his story would end up while he was in the middle of it, but he persevered, remained faithful to God, and sought God's will.

Logos vs. Rhema

Concepts in the following section are based primarily on teaching from Delron Shirley[15]. My brief study of the words *logos* and *rhema* in my Key Word Bible[16] seem to support Delron's teaching.

Before leaving this chapter and part 2 of this book, let's talk about the concept of logos versus rhema.

In the Bible, there are two words in the Greek for the word *word*. Logos means a general understanding or collection of principles, such as those available to anyone who reads the Bible. Rhema refers to a specific Word from God for each one of us to address the specific questions and issues that we face every day.

I've heard it said, and I agree, that by learning and applying the principles found in God's Word (logos), each and every one of us can enter into a relationship with God that will include a specific revelation of a rhema that will help guide our daily decisions and choices.

For some of us, God wants us to become missionaries. For some of us, we are exactly where God wants us to be in the job that we have right now.

How can we know that rhema, that timely Word from God, just for us, about how and where He wants us to spend our working hours? How do we know if we are in the exact occupation God wants us to be?

As we discussed in the last chapter, I believe this process begins by earnestly seeking God. One very tangible way to do this is to consistently read and meditate on the Bible. By doing so, we'll begin to know the mind of Christ about a number of issues related to our work and our career. When it comes to our work, we can then begin to think like Jesus.

In part 3, beginning with the next chapter, we'll start to do just that.

PART 3

Think Like Jesus

No one knows the things of God except the Spirit of God. Now we have received, not the spirit of the world, but the Spirit who is from God, that we might know the things that have been freely given to us by God... But we have the mind of Christ.

—1 Corinthians 2:11, 12, 16 (NKJV)

What Jesus Thinks About Work

And the Lord God took the man, and put him into the garden of Eden to dress it and to keep it.

—Genesis 2:15 (KJV)

Work is important. One demonstration of that is how much God has to say about it.

One search online showed the word *work* occurs 401 times in 374 verses in the NKJV[17] and the word *labor* occurs 109 times in 105 verses in the NKJV[18].

From a sampling of these verses, I have drawn at least five conclusions, or truths, regarding this topic of work.

God is a Worker

The Bible shows that God has always been a worker and been about His work.

"And on the seventh day God ended His work which He had done, and He rested on the seventh day from all His work which He had done." (Genesis 2:2 NKJV)

Exactly what kind of work had God been up to? As the first chapter of Genesis tells us, God was creating the universe! Since God never changes (Malachi 3:6) and He is eternal, with no beginning and no end (John 1:1), we can assume that He didn't just start working when He decided to create the world. He has always been a worker and always will be.

When Jesus healed the man by the pool of Bethesda, he was criticized for doing so on the Sabbath. But Jesus answered them, "My Father has been working until now, and I have been working." (John 5:17 NKJV)

"Working until now"—Yes, that sounds like someone who has always been working to me.

Another example of God's nature as continuously working is found in the book of Philippians: "he which hath begun a good work in you will perform it until the day of Jesus Christ:" (Philippians 1:6 KJV)

Not only does God continue to work on our behalf, but He was doing so long before we were even conceived in our mother's womb.

"Your eyes saw my substance, being yet unformed. And in Your book they all were written, The days fashioned for me, When *as yet there were* none of them" (Psalm 139:16 NKJV)

Hopefully that does a lot for your self-image and gives you a different outlook on whether work is a good thing, which is the next truth.

Work Is Good

In the first chapter of Genesis, we see that with each step of God's work of creating the universe, He proclaimed it to be *good*. God didn't do this work out of obligation. It was His choice, and He was pleased with the results.

It didn't take long before He showed that He wanted man to join Him in working.

"And the Lord God took the man, and put him into the garden of Eden to dress it and to keep it." (Genesis 2:15 kjv)

This was enjoyable, satisfying, meaningful work, the way God intended it to be. Later, Adam and Eve ate the forbidden fruit and God told Adam, "Because thou hast hearkened unto the voice of thy wife, and hast eaten of the tree, of which I commanded thee, saying, Thou shalt not eat of it: cursed is the ground for thy sake; in sorrow shalt thou eat of it all the days of thy life; Thorns also and thistles shall it bring forth to thee; and thou shalt eat the herb of the field; In the sweat of thy face shalt thou eat bread, till thou return unto the ground; for out of it wast thou taken: for dust thou art, and unto dust shalt thou return." (Genesis 3:17-19 kjv)

It's clear that God originally created work to be good. The question is, is our work today good or is it cursed? I've struggled with an adequate answer to this question but have concluded that our work today is good for several reasons.

- God did not actually curse work in response to Adam's sin, but rather he cursed the ground, resulting in additional work required to work the ground. You can certainly argue that this curse applied to all work, but I believe that if God meant it to be applied to all work He would have said so.

- It's possible that this curse was lifted after the flood. When Noah left the ark, he built an altar to the Lord "and the Lord said in his heart, I will not again curse the ground any more for man's sake; for the imagination of man's heart is evil from his youth; neither will I again smite any more every thing living, as I have done." (Genesis 8:21 KJV)
- When Jesus died and rose from the dead, He gave every one of us the potential to become new creations. "Therefore if any man be in Christ, he is a new creature: old things are passed away; behold, all things are become new." (2 Corinthians 5:17 KJV)

In Galatians, Paul writes, "Christ hath redeemed us from the curse of the law, being made a curse for us: for it is written, Cursed is every one that hangeth on a tree:" (Galatians 3:13 KJV)

My understanding is that when Paul refers to "the Law" he is referring to the Old Testament, not just the law given to Moses. If that's true, then any curse handed out in the Old Testament is now removed.

I don't have all the answers to these questions surrounding work as being good, and I encourage you to do your own study. I think it's clear that God's work creating the universe as well as God's original work intended for man was good, and I believe that ever since Christ died and rose again, work for believers has had the potential to be what it was intended to be, before the fall, which was very good.

God Wants Us to Work

Not only do we see that God has always been a worker and that He values work as good, the Bible also shows that God wants for us to work. This makes sense given that God's nature is to want what is best for us.

In Ephesians, Paul writes,

"For we are his workmanship, created in Christ Jesus unto good works, which God hath before ordained that we should walk in them." (Ephesians 2:10 kjv)

Many people don't realize there's actually a commandment to work in the Ten Commandments. The commandment to remember the Sabbath and keep it holy begins with a command to work: "Six days shalt thou labour, and do all thy work: But the seventh day is the sabbath of the Lord thy God" (Exodus 20:9-10 kjv)

Jesus reminded us how much work is available to those in His kingdom: "Then He said to His disciples, 'The harvest truly *is* plentiful, but the laborers *are* few.'" (Matthew 9:37 nkjv).

On the other hand, *not* working is associated with a number of negative things in the Bible. "If anyone will not work, neither shall he eat." (2 Thessalonians 3:10 nkjv).

There's Wisdom in Work

There are a number of benefits to working, including:

- Have Better Sleep—"The sleep of a laboring man *is* sweet, Whether he eats little or much; But the abundance of the rich will not permit him to sleep." (Ecclesiastes 5:12 nkjv)

- Establish Your Thoughts—"Commit your works to the Lord, and your thoughts will be established." (Proverbs 16:3 NKJV)
- Improve Your Company—"Do you see a man *who* excels in his work? He will stand before kings; He will not stand before unknown *men*" (Proverbs 22:29 NKJV)
- Provide For Your Family and Receive Praise From Them—"She seeks wool and flax, And willingly works with her hands. She also rises while it is yet night, And provides food for her household, And a portion for her maidservants. She watches over the ways of her household, And does not eat the bread of idleness. Her children rise up and call her blessed; Her husband *also,* and he praises her: 'Many daughters have done well, But you excel them all.'" (Proverbs 31:13, 15, 27-29, NKJV)
- Give To Others—"She extends her hand to the poor, Yes, she reaches out her hands to the needy." (Proverbs 31:20 NKJV)
- Get Fed and Be Honored—"Whoever keeps the fig tree will eat its fruit; So he who waits on his master will be honored." (Proverbs 27:18 NKJV)
- Earn a Profit—"In all labor there is profit, But idle chatter *leads* only to poverty." (Proverbs 14:23 NKJV)

God is Our Boss

After Jesus miraculously fed thousands with just five loaves of bread and two fish, He told the disciples, "Do not labor for the food which perishes, but for the food which endures to everlasting life, which the Son of Man will give you, because God the Father has set His seal on Him." (John 6:27 NKJV)

In Ephesians and in Colossians, Paul powerfully reminds us that no matter whom we serve on earth, ultimately we are serving the Lord and that we show our reverence to Him by the way we serve our earthly masters (bosses).

> Bondservants, obey in all things your masters according to the flesh, not with eyeservice, as men-pleasers, but in sincerity of heart, fearing God. And whatever you do, do it heartily, as to the Lord and not to men, knowing that from the Lord you will receive the reward of the inheritance; for you serve the Lord Christ.
>
> Colossians 3:22-24 (NKJV)

Notice the emphasis is not just on serving, but serving with a positive attitude. We should not just work and work well, but we should do so "in sincerity of heart."

God Cares about Our Work

We know that God is with us all the time (see Deuteronomy 31:8), and since we spend a lot of our time at work, it follows that God is with us every minute of our workday. We also know that God had a plan for us even before we were conceived (Psalm 139:16) and that He cares about us so much He knows how many hairs are on our heads (Matthew 10:30 and Luke 12:7).

It naturally follows, then, that He cares about what's going on with us at our job. If God cares so much about our work, we probably should too.

Unfortunately, both Christians and non–Christians make the mistake of not valuing our work as God does. Instead, they often just think of their job as a way to make money, nothing more and nothing less. Since that is such a common view, we probably should take a look at what the Bible has to say about money as well.

We'll do that in our next chapter.

What Jesus Thinks About Money

God has given us more than 2,350 verses in the Bible to instruct us in how to be good stewards of what God has placed in our care, making it second to the subject of love as the most discussed subject in the Bible. In fact, two-thirds of the parables that Jesus taught are about money, possessions, and stewardship.

Taken from http://www.crown.org

God must know that money is and will continue to be a big part of our lives, or I don't think He would have included so many verses in the Bible related to money.

Money is too broad of a topic to adequately cover in one chapter, but it's too important and too closely related to our work for me to neglect it entirely in this book.

In the first part of this chapter I'm going to touch on several issues related to money that I think are particularly important because they impact how we manage our money as well as how we think about money. In the last part of the chapter, I'm going to speak to the question of whether God wants us to prosper financially.

I'm going to be dealing with concepts here. If you want a plan, step-by-step instructions, on how to manage your money in a biblical way, I strongly recommend you check out Dave Ramsey. Read his book *Financial Peace Revisited*[19] and then take his class *Financial Peace University*[20].

The lives of me and my wife were changed dramatically for the better after we took *FPU* through a home group in our church in 2007, implemented his plan into our daily lives, and then facilitated an FPU class in 2012. I'm excited to say we're going to facilitate another class in the next few months.

Tithing and Giving

I believe strongly that the Bible commands us to tithe, to give 10% of all of our income to our local church.

> "Will a man rob God?
> Yet you have robbed Me!
> But you say,
> 'In what way have we robbed You?'
> In tithes and offerings.
> You are cursed with a curse,
> For you have robbed Me,
> *Even* this whole nation
> Bring all the tithes into the storehouse,
> That there may be food in My house,
> And try Me now in this,"
> Says the Lord of hosts,
> "If I will not open for you the windows of heaven

And pour out for you *such* blessing
That *there will* not *be room* enough *to receive it.*
"And I will rebuke the devourer for your sakes,
So that he will not destroy the fruit of your ground,
Nor shall the vine fail to bear fruit for you in the field,"
Says the LORD of hosts;

(Malachi 3:8-11 NKJV)

Abraham tithed before the law was given to Moses (see Genesis 14:19-21). Therefore I believe tithing is relevant for all believers in every generation.

I think it's interesting that God doesn't just command us to tithe, He asks us to *test* Him.

Why would He do that? I believe it's because He wants to bless all of us financially, but He wants us to do our part and cooperate with the laws He has established regarding money. My pastor suggested (and I agree) that the reason God says "you have robbed Me" in Malachi 3:8 is because by not tithing we are robbing Him of the opportunity to bless us![21]

Can or will God bless us financially whether or not we are obedient to Him regarding what He's told us to do in the Bible with money? The answer to that question gets into a whole area of doctrine regarding the sovereignty of God, which is beyond the scope of this book. Having said that, if you're a parent or ever have been, I challenge you to think about how you've handled this issue of money with your own kids. Have you showered your children with blessings every time they've done foolish things that, if repeated, would only lead to hurt and destruction for them and others? Probably not. I haven't either. I think we're acting like our Daddy.

My personal testimony is that ever since my wife and I committed to tithing for the rest of our lives, God has been pouring out blessings on us just like He said He would in Malachi 3:8-11. We've had more than enough for our needs and our wants as well as extra to give to other ministries and people in need.

If you're a child of God, you are made in His image and you should want to be like your Daddy. He's the ultimate giver (John 3:16). Just as you want your child to be like you and think like you (at least the good parts), God wants us to be like Him, and this includes being a giver.

I believe this whole issue of tithing and giving is relevant to our work because it gets right to the heart of whose money it is in the first place. Your paycheck is a gift from God, not something you earned separate from Him. Knowing that should change your whole attitude toward your work for the better.

Personal Debt

The teaching from Dave Ramsey's FPU course that probably had the biggest impact on me was in the area of personal debt.

Dave taught me how the use of personal debt, including the use of credit cards, is not biblical and is a fairly recent change in behavior in our society.

He also showed me how stupid it is to go into debt and how debt keeps us in bondage financially as well as emotionally.

"The rich ruleth over the poor, and the borrower is servant to the lender." (Proverbs 22:7 KJV).

"Owe no one anything except to love one another, for he who loves another has fulfilled the law." (Romans 13:8 NKJV)

My wife and I will never use a credit card again and we're debt free other than what remains on our home mortgage. I highly recommend it!

Being a Good Steward

A steward is a person who manages another's property or financial affairs; one who administers anything as the agent of another or others[22]

My own definition of a good steward is someone who values highly, and makes the most of, what they are asked to be responsible for.

Stewardship is perhaps dealt with best in the parable of the talents in the book of Matthew. In that parable, Jesus likened the kingdom of God to a man who entrusts three of his servants with some money while he's away. When he returns, he lavishes praise on the two servants who doubled the money they'd originally been given. "'Well *done*, good and faithful servant; you have been faithful over a few things, I will make you ruler over many things. Enter into the joy of your lord.'" (Matthew 25:23 NKJV)

The third servant, however, who'd been given the smallest amount of money and chose to hide the money rather than invest it, received a particularly harsh response:

> You wicked and lazy servant… take the talent from him, and give *it* to him who has ten talents. For to everyone who has, more will be given, and he will have abundance; but from him who does not have,

even what he has will be taken away. And cast the unprofitable servant into the outer darkness. There will be weeping and gnashing of teeth.

Matthew 25:26, 28–30 (nkjv)

One lesson I've taken from this parable is that it's an honor and a blessing to be asked to be a steward. That's true whenever God blesses us financially and with a job. It's also true when we are blessed with time, abilities, people, and opportunities. To me, God seems to also be telling us through the sharp contrast between the master's responses to the three servants how important it is to Him that we do a good job as stewards once He has blessed us and entrusted us with His blessings.

I believe that what we do with what we've been given matters to God, and it should matter to us as well.

Providing is a Noble Aspect of Your Work

For most people, money is primarily, if not entirely, what their work is all about.

Lacking a divine purpose and assignment for their career, they're left thinking of their work as a necessary evil, a means to an end. "I owe, I owe, so off to work I go." The meaning for their job is then boiled down to a paycheck every two weeks, nothing more and nothing less. In other words, their work is equated only with their financial needs and goals. Hopefully once you're done reading this book, you'll agree with what the Bible says, that our work is about much more than finances.

Having said that, it would be a mistake to say that our work has *nothing* to do with our finances; it certainly does. In fact, the Bible uses some strong language to show that one reason for work is to provide for our families and meet our financial obligations, and by itself that is a good and worthy thing.

"But if anyone does not provide for his own, and especially for those of his household, he has denied the faith and is worse than an unbeliever." (1 Timothy 5:8 NKJV)

What exactly does the Bible mean by providing? Should we only be striving to meet our basic needs (food, shelter, clothing), or is it okay to include in our definition of provision other nonessentials—things that are better than average, even luxurious? In other words, is it okay to include our wants as well as our needs in our financial goals?

Or take it a step further, is it okay (or even a good thing) to be rich or to seek wealth? What does God think when we include these kinds of financial goals in such life decisions as our career choices, our attitude toward our work, and the priority work holds in our lives?

The Greek word for *provide* used in 1 Timothy 5:8 is *pronoeo*, which means "to consider in advance," i.e., "look out for beforehand"[23]. To how far in advance does this definition of *provide* refer (today, tomorrow, next week, twenty years)?

The book of Proverbs offers some insight into these questions.

"A good *man* leaves an inheritance to his children's children" (Proverbs 13:22 NKJV)

Certainly leaving an inheritance to not just your children but your grandchildren requires more than just earning enough to pay today's bills or to meet the basic necessities of life. *"There is* desirable treasure, And oil in the dwelling of the wise, But a foolish man squanders it." (Proverbs 21:20 NKJV)

There are many examples of leaders in the Bible, including Abraham, Isaac, Jacob, David, Solomon, and Joseph of Arimathea, who were financially blessed by God and as a result were very wealthy. They each had an important role in carrying out God's plan on this earth, and their wealth was a factor in them playing their part.

It's clear to me that God does not view financial wealth, in and of itself, to be a bad thing or something we should intentionally avoid. I also think that God uses our financial wealth to carry out His purposes.

Since there is a clear connection between our work and our ability to earn money and provide for ourselves and others, I think it's safe to say, then, that one way we are living out our assignment from God through our work is by earning money and acquiring wealth.

Money's Not the Problem

As soon as you start to talk about wealth as a good thing or God's will, you're sure to raise cries of foul from many in the body of Christ. I've been in churches and heard from teachers across the spectrum on this issue. I've heard the word *prosperity* spoken of as God's will for all of us, and I've heard the word *prosperity*, or more specifically a *prosperity gospel*, used in a hateful and derogatory way from the pulpit.

What is the correct way to think about money? It's an important question for which I believe we all need to be clear where we stand. You can't just say you're not sure; it's too important of an issue to ignore.

Like everything in life, the answer, the sweet spot, for this question of how we should think about money, is found in Scripture.

Perhaps the most famous reference to money in the Bible is 1 Timothy 6:10, which is often misquoted as "money is the root of all evil." The correct version is,

"For the love of money is the root of all *kinds of* evil, for which some have strayed from the faith in their greediness, and pierced themselves through with many sorrows." (1 Timothy 6:10 NKJV)

Verse 9 just before this issues an even stronger warning: "But those who desire to be rich fall into temptation and a snare, and *into* many foolish and harmful lusts which drown men in destruction and perdition." (1 Timothy 6:9 NKJV)

"*Let your* conduct *be* without covetousness; *be* content with such things as you have. For He Himself has said, "I will never leave you nor forsake you." (Hebrews 13:5 NKJV)

So the problem, the evil, is not money itself but rather the love of money. The danger of loving money is that it can lead to idolatry. By focusing too much or relying too much on money and the things that it buys, we begin to lose our dependence on our Creator and instead start to rely on His creation.

We begin to look to earthly things, such as our job, as our provider, when in reality God is our provider. He just uses earthly things like our job as a means of His provision.

"Command those who are rich in this present age not to be haughty, nor to trust in uncertain riches but in the living God, who gives us richly all things to enjoy." (1 Timothy 6:17 NKJV)

Remember the last part of Hebrews 13:5: "I will never leave you nor forsake you." (Hebrews 13:5 NKJV)

God will always be there for us and take care of us, no matter what. The Holy Spirit may have included the last part of this passage because our sense of insecurity in this life, which should draw us closer to and more dependent upon God, instead oftentimes draws us to money and the things of this world. We define our financial security in human terms (a big bank account, a high net worth, a stable job) rather than in spiritual terms.

Jesus advised us in what we call His Sermon on the Mount to be careful selecting the type of treasures we store while we're here.

"Do not lay up for yourselves treasures on earth, where moth and rust destroy and where thieves break in and steal; but lay up for yourselves treasures in heaven, where neither moth nor rust destroys and where thieves do not break in and steal. For where your treasure is, there your heart will be also." (Matthew 6:19-21 NKJV)

Don't Let Your Stuff Have You

You may have heard it said that it's okay to have money (or stuff) as long as the money (stuff) doesn't have you. That's a catchy saying, but is this really that big of a deal to guard against letting money control us? The answer, apparently, is yes, that is, if you want to be a disciple of Jesus.

First of all, what does it mean to be a disciple? One definition is "one who accepts and assists in spreading the doctrines of another"[24]

In Luke chapter 14, Jesus describes several tests required for being one of His disciples:

- Hating your relatives and your own life
- Carrying your own cross and coming after Him
- Planning ahead of time what the cost of discipleship will be so you are ready

(paraphrased from Luke 14:26–32 NKJV)

He summarizes all these tests by saying in verse 33: "So likewise, whoever of you does not forsake all that he has cannot be My disciple." (Luke 14:33, NKJV)

The Greek word translated as *forsake* is *apotassomai*. In this verse it is used figuratively[25]. Just as with His comment that we should hate our relatives and our own life, I believe Jesus didn't mean this literally but rather figuratively. He wasn't saying we had to physically give up all of our possessions, but rather that it was necessary to do so in spirit. In other words, even if you don't give up all your physical possessions, be sincerely willing to do so because your relationship with your Savior has a higher priority in your life than any material thing you have acquired.

In other words, don't let your stuff have you.

When the rich man asked Jesus how to get to heaven, Jesus listed several commandments he needed to obey. The man foolishly and naively said he had always kept those (impossible—no one who has lived on this earth other than Jesus can honestly make such a claim).

"Then Jesus, looking at him, loved him, and said to him, 'One thing you lack: Go your way, sell whatever you have and give to the poor, and you will have treasure in heaven; and come, take up the cross, and follow Me.'" (Mark 10:21 NKJV)

Does this mean the rich man literally needed to sell all he had in order to go to heaven, or that we have to do the same? Well, let me start to answer that question by stating that the wonderful message of the Gospel is that we are saved only by God's grace through faith that Jesus Christ died on the cross to save us from our sins (see Ephesians 2:8–9, John 3:16, Romans 10:9–10, Romans 6:23, Titus 3:5–6). I believe Jesus was challenging the man to be willing to give up his idol—the material things that he valued more than he did Jesus. God wants our whole heart.

In three separate Gospels, Jesus says, "it is easier for a camel to go through the eye of a needle, than for a rich man to enter the kingdom of God." (Matthew 19:24, Mark 10:25, Luke 18:25 NKJV)

After His disciples questioned who then could be saved, Jesus replied "With men *it is* impossible, but not with God; for with God all things are possible." (Mark 10:27 NKJV)

I've heard a variety of explanations of what Jesus meant by these verses. I encourage you to research this on your own, but I believe at a minimum the following conclusions can be made from what Jesus said.

- The kingdom of God offers infinitely more to us than our earthly riches.
- It is impossible (not just difficult) for a rich person, more specifically someone who trusts in

their riches more than they trust God, to enter into the kingdom of God.

- Only God by supernatural means can change this situation by drawing men to Him instead of the things of this world.

Don't Let Your Mistakes Skew Your View of Money

You may not be able to relate to this, but there was a time in my life when money was my god and the pursuit of it was my passion. Because of the destruction that misguided thinking brought to my life, I have a tendency to think of money itself as a bad thing and to question whether God wants me to prosper financially.

At those times, I'm reminded[26] of the following verses:

> Let them shout for joy and be glad,
> Who favor my righteous cause;
> And let them say continually,
> "Let the Lord be magnified,
> Who has pleasure in the prosperity of His servant."
>
> Psalm 35:27 NKJV

> "The LORD *is* my shepherd; I shall not want."
>
> Psalm 23:1 NKJV

> God "gives us richly all things to enjoy."
>
> 1 Timothy 6:17 NKJV

Praise the Lord!
Blessed *is* the man *who* fears the Lord,
Who delights greatly in His commandments.
His descendants will be mighty on earth;
The generation of the upright will be blessed.
Wealth and riches *will be* in his house,
And his righteousness endures forever.

Psalm 112:1-3 NKJV

The Bottom Line

Solomon was the wisest man to ever live on earth, short of Jesus. He also is arguably the richest man in human history. After having it all, he wrote at length in the book of Ecclesiastes about the folly of relying on riches for happiness.

"He who loves silver will not be satisfied with silver; Nor he who loves abundance, with increase. This also *is* vanity." (Ecclesiastes 5:10 NKJV)

If money, or the pursuit of it, doesn't provide a purpose or happiness, and if most people consider the primary reason for their work to be making money, it's no wonder so many people are unhappy and unsatisfied with their work, and their life.

The overriding theme from the Bible regarding money seems to me to be:

- There's nothing inherently wrong with money, or with having money
- God wants to bless us financially so that we can be blessed and so that we can be a blessing to

others. I like what my pastor says: "God wants us to have plenty so we can be a blessing to many"[27]

- We should make sure that money does not become our idol and the best way to do this is to be focused on God above everything else.

A simple comparison illustrates this well. Although Jesus told one rich man he needed to sell all his possessions (Mark 10:21), he didn't say the same thing to another rich man, Zaccheus (Luke 19:1–10). The difference seems to be that Zaccheus demonstrated through his actions that money was no longer his god.

God loves us so much and wants us to have good things. In fact, it's only through God's blessings that we can have wealth, or things, and actually enjoy them rather than always lusting for more.

"The blessing of the LORD makes *one* rich, And He adds no sorrow with it." (Proverbs 10:22 NKJV)

There are plenty of things that look like blessings in life but ultimately have a bunch of sorrow added to them. Praise God that His blessings have no strings attached!

"As for every man to whom God has given riches and wealth, and given him power to eat of it, to receive his heritage and rejoice in his labor—this *is* the gift of God." (Ecclesiastes 5:19 NKJV)

God created us in order to have a relationship with us. As our perfect Friend (see Isaiah 41:8, John 15:15) and Father (see Luke 11:11–13), He wants us to have good things. Since He knows the best possible thing we can have is to be in communion with Him, something that cannot be purchased with money, it makes sense that He would not want us to be distracted from that relationship by money.

However, He's a gentleman. He didn't make us to be robots, and He won't force a relationship with Him onto us. At the same time, He's not going to give us things if He knows we aren't able to have those blessings without being drawn away from the much greater and ultimate blessing, a personal relationship with Him.

God did not intend for our lives to boil down to what we can obtain and collect for ourselves or how much fun we can have while we're here. Our purpose, rather, is to be found in Him, with Him, and in His purposes. In doing so, we will find everything we ever wanted, and much more.

Jesus said "But seek first the kingdom of God and His righteousness, and all these things shall be added to you." (Matthew 6:33 NKJV)

I think that's my favorite passage about money of all, even though it doesn't actually contain a direct reference to money. What a wonderful description of a loving God and what a simple life formula He's given for us to follow. We can seek His kingdom right where we are no matter what our income level and no matter what type of work we do, but only if we have the proper perspective of money and work.

That leads us to our next chapter. We're going to dig into the concept that despite what you may think, you are, in fact, already a missionary; and as you seek His kingdom, you need look no further than your current circumstances and your current job to find that kingdom.

You're Already a Missionary

You are now entering the mission field.

—(sign at the exit from a church
somewhere in Florida)

My family and I were leaving my parents' church in Florida one Sunday and we saw an interesting sign as we turned out of the church parking lot. "You are now entering the mission field," it said. I smiled at the clever sign as I pondered the truth in its message.

Ministry Redefined

Many people make the mistake of thinking that the only people who are truly working for God and have a divine assignment for their work are those in full-time ministry. Their definition of full-time ministry is typically limited to clergymen, pastors, foreign missionaries, and those preaching or ministering God's Word through TV, books, music, and the like.

I believe it's a mistake to think this way for a number of reasons.

Jesus Didn't Say So

On several occasions, Jesus spoke with those in secular occupations but didn't tell them they needed to quit and become a full-time minister.

In Luke 19:1–10, Jesus visits the home of Zaccheus, who was a tax collector, also referred to as a publican.

"Publicans were held in the lowest esteem because of their excessive profits, being placed in the same category as harlots. (Matthew 21:32)"[28]. Despite the fact that tax collecting had such a bad reputation, as far as we know, Jesus never told Zaccheus to quit his job.

At one point, Jesus meets a centurion and says, "I have not found such a great faith, not even in Israel!" (Matthew 8:10 NKJV). There's no indication Jesus felt it was necessary to tell this centurion to leave his job.

When Jesus said on many occasions "follow me", I believe He wanted us to be willing to leave any earthly thing in our life to follow Him. This certainly includes our job. We should be willing to leave our job and, if at some point we know that God's will is for us to leave our job, we should certainly do so; but if we're not certain that is God's will, in my opinion we should stay right where we are.

I think it's worth noting that Jesus didn't ask one tax collector, Zaccheus, to quit his job, but he did ask another tax collector, Matthew, to quit his job and follow Him as one of His disciples (see Matthew 9:9).

The difference was not in their occupations; they were the same. The difference was in the calling Jesus had for each of their lives.

You're in a Unique Position

Another reason I think it's a mistake to limit our concept of full-time ministry is that no matter what our occupation is, we are in a unique and often favorable position to minister to others.

I've heard pastors say on several occasions that those of us who are not in full-time ministry are oftentimes in a better position to reach and minister to others for two main reasons.

First, we know people that our pastors don't know and will never know. The reason is obvious; we're out in the world working and doing things our pastors don't do, and as a result we're interacting with people to whom they don't have access.

Just think about it for a moment. Think of all the people you know and with whom you can make an impact, particularly at work since you spend so much time there. Most of those people will probably never hear of or meet your pastor, or maybe even *any* pastor. But they do know *you*, and they see you and hear from you every day. They're paying attention to what you say and what you do. You may be the best representative they have of the church (the body of Christ) in their lives, and as a result you have a huge responsibility and opportunity to make a difference to them.

The second reason I've heard from pastors that we are in a better position than they are to reach and minister to others is because the people we meet, know, work with, and interact with on a daily basis are generally more at ease around us than they are around full-time ministers.

One of my former pastors, Dave Stewart, shared a story when he was on a plane speaking with someone who began opening up to Pastor Dave about his life and his struggles[29].

I don't know how much you've traveled in your life, but I've done this enough to be able to relate to this story. Sitting alone on a long flight with no one else nearby and no other distractions other than the noise of the engines can be a great opportunity to get to know someone, even if it's just for a short time. Sometimes you find yourself opening up to a stranger under these circumstances (or find someone opening up to you) in ways that would not feel comfortable under normal circumstances.

That was the case with Pastor Dave. His new friend was comfortable enough to open up about some things in his life that were really troubling him, and for which he really needed ministry and comfort.

Unfortunately, as soon as the man found out he was speaking with a full-time minister, his demeanor changed and not for the better. Once he knew he was with a *man of the cloth*, he instinctively became more reserved, more careful about what he said, and less open to be helped and comforted.

Oftentimes, people will put on a show for a pastor and act all spiritual, but they'll be more sincere, more real, and have more of an open heart with someone to whom they can more easily relate.

In addition, the testimony of a layperson can be more powerful than that of a preacher. The other person may think, *Well, he's just like me, living and working in the real world, going through the same struggles I am (or worse), and yet he's on fire for God, and look at the fruit in his life!*

Jesus said, "I do not ask You to take them out of the world, but to keep them from the evil one." (John 17:15 NKJV)

Just as a fisherman can't sit at home if he wants to catch fish but rather needs to find a spot in the water where the fish are present, in the same way we need to be in the world, at our job, while at the same time not be *of* the world.

Your pastor can't be everywhere you are every day, and even if he or she could be, they might not be as effective as you.

Lose the Guilt Trip

Yet another reason it's a mistake to have the wrong idea about full-time ministry is that it can lead you to feel unnecessary and misplaced guilt, regret, and stress for having made a career choice you think is outside of God's will. I can relate to this because I've felt this way in the past; and on a day when I let my emotions rule me, I can briefly feel that way still today.

I also know about this because I've heard from so many other Christians this sense of guilt and regret.

This can then lead to a number of negative consequences for you and your life.

First, it can cause you to lose your appreciation and your enthusiasm for your work and career. This in turn can steal your joy and make you less effective at what you do. It can also cause you to miss out on all that God has planned for you through your work.

Second, feeling guilty about not being in what you consider to be full-time ministry may lead you to try to overcompensate by becoming over-involved in a variety of ministries through your church or some other organization outside of your work.

I certainly am not against getting involved in your church or helping others whenever you can. The Bible encourages us to be in community with fellow believers and to help others, and I believe that is part of growing and maturing in our faith.

As with the story of Kevin the mechanic, though, I think sometimes people are motivated to serve, at least partially, for the wrong reasons. As a result, they end up feeling the same emptiness or lack of divine purpose in their volunteer or ministry efforts as they feel in their job, and at the same time may feel guilty about neglecting other areas of their life. The devil really has a heyday when he has us feeling guilty and unsatisfied with all aspects of our lives.

I've certainly made this mistake in the past, doing good in an attempt to stop feeling bad, when God never wanted me to feel bad in the first place. The result was I felt even worse and even less satisfied because I was in a works mentality—trying to earn God's favor when Jesus had already earned it for me.

As we discussed in the chapter *What Jesus Thinks about Work*, God does want us to work, and that work can certainly include volunteering and helping others outside of our primary job. I believe, however, that God also wants us to take time to develop a relationship with Him, with our families, and with others.

If we fill up every waking hour outside of our job with volunteer commitments, we won't leave any time for the other important people and activities in our lives. This is particularly true if we're doing it for the wrong reasons like trying to satisfy misplaced guilt.

I believe that God does in fact have a perfect job in mind for us just as He has an opinion on every single choice and decision we have in our lives. If we goof up, though, and pick the wrong career, I believe God is still pleased with us and we still can please Him and have a fulfilling and God-pleasing life and career. We can do that by seeking His will for the job He wants for us and pursuing that job, but we don't have to wait for a job change to be at peace with God and have fulfillment in our work.

In fact, I believe that almost regardless what our career is, each of us has just as much of an opportunity, or more, to have a divine purpose and to serve God as does Billy Graham or any other person you think of as being in full-time ministry.

The Pitfall of Tomorrow Thinking

One of the biggest mistakes we can make is to put off until tomorrow what God wants for us today.

As we've been discussing, one form of what I would call "tomorrow thinking" is when we put off a life devoted to God until we are in the type of career that we consider to be "spiritually acceptable."

Another form of tomorrow thinking is when we put off our joy and purpose for an entire working career, in anticipation of our retirement.

I believe this second type of tomorrow thinking can be a real problem, particularly among non-Christians but also with some Christians. We'll focus on that issue in the next chapter.

Think Differently about Retirement

> Beware lest anyone cheat you through philosophy
> and empty deceit, according to the tradition of
> men, according to the basic principles of the
> world, and not according to Christ.
>
> —Colossians 2:8 (NKJV)

In this chapter, I want to talk about the best attitude to have regarding retirement.

I want to enter into this conversation with care and humility.

First, I'm about 20 years short of what is typically considered retirement age. As such, I have not been in the shoes, so to speak, of either those of you who are nearing retirement, nor those of you who are already retired.

Second, unlike many of the topics in this book, I don't have a great number of scripture references from which to form a solid opinion on this topic.

Despite my hesitancy, I decided to include this in the book and have the conversation because I think our attitude toward our retirement will have a big impact on how we act and think about our work today, throughout our entire career, and for the rest of our lives.

I want to thank my friend, Dr. Marion Griffin[30], for the frank insight he gave me on this topic of retirement after he read through my manuscript prior to publishing. His thoughts are reflected throughout this chapter.

My interest in this topic was first peaked when I read a book by Larry Burkett called *Preparing for Retirement*.

Thought I don't agree with everything he writes in his book, I believe Larry Burkett sums up very well the history behind a significant change in attitude in our society toward retirement, as well as the scriptural basis for what he views to be a correct attitude about retirement,

> I am convinced that retirement, as we know it in our generation, is not scriptural. I'm not implying that someone who retires at age 62 or 65 is living in sin. There are some instances where retirement is a part of God's plan for a particular individual. But the basic concept of idling the majority of people at such an early age is a modern innovation, not a biblical principle.
>
> There is actually only one direct reference to retirement in the Bible: "This is what applies to the Levites: from twenty-five years old and upward they should enter to perform service in the work of the tent of meeting. But at the age of fifty years they shall retire from service in the work and not work any more." (Numbers 8:24-25)
>
> Exactly why God directed that the priests should retire at 50 is not known. It is possible that they assisted in other functions but could not

perform the ceremonies themselves. So if you're a Levite priest, according to God's Word your retirement decisions have been made. If you're not, read on.

Retirement, as we know it, is so new that most current retirees can still remember when practically no one retired. In my grandfather's generation certainly few, if any, ordinary citizens would have seriously considered that they could stop working and play golf at 65 or so.

In the first place, few Americans made enough money to be able to retire to the golf course. And those who did were so committed to their careers that they had little interest in retirement.

For our present system of retirement to function, two essential elements are required: first, a large class of workers who make sufficient incomes to save a sizeable portion for the future; and second, most of these workers must be so dissatisfied with their jobs that they're willing to quit at an early age.

Such a combination was found in two groups of workers during the fifties: union members and federal employees. As the labor unions grew in number and strength during the high employment period after World War II, their collective bargaining eventually took in long-term benefits, such as retirement. Companies were more than willing to negotiate for deferred benefits in lieu of current wage increases.

For the first time, retirement became an attainable goal for blue collar workers. The impact this idea was to have on American society was incalculable at that time. It would eventually give rise to a multi-billion dollar investment industry in the sixties, and would doom the Social Security system to failure as the majority of workers over sixty decided they could retire.

Once the retirement "bandwagon" got rolling, millions of additional people joined it. Eventually American workers became convinced that retirement is a basic "right." During the sixties and seventies laws were passed requiring workers to retire by age 65. With more and more younger workers coming into the work force, retirement became a logical way to free up jobs.

…The basic issue I am addressing here is not the Social Security system; nor is it whether individuals can save enough to stop work at 62 and live comfortably. The real issue is: Is retirement itself a biblical principal God established for His people?

Since there is so little Scripture dealing with this subject, it would seem logical to make one of two assumptions: Either God forgot to discuss the subject of retirement, or it is not a part of His plan for us. I discovered long ago that God doesn't forget anything; therefore it has to be that our whole perspective of retirement is out of balance.

…Retirement is not *prohibited,* it simply is not discussed to any degree. Therefore it is little more than an innovative way for modern society to escape the drudgery of work-place boredom.

…Remember: God uniquely created each of us, including our endurance and durability and, as a result, not everyone will have the same ability to work at the various stages of life. Consequently, there will be varying degrees of retirement for all of us. The degree to which we slow down is not the fundamental issue here; ceasing all productive activity is.

...God in His infinite wisdom knew that His creation would need rest and relaxation. The method He chose to provide that rest and relaxation is called a sabbatical – the resting time. The term sabbatical comes from Sabbath, or the day of rest in each week.

In the fifth chapter of Deuteronomy, the Lord told the Jews that they should work six days, but *"the seventh day is a Sabbath..."* The meaning behind the Sabbath is two-fold: The first is to set apart a day to honor the Lord; the second is to take a day a week to rest and recover. This practice was extended to include a sabbath year, called the year of remission, described in Deuteronomy 15:1-11.

This is not a book for an in-depth discussion of the sabbath day. Rather, I want to point out that God has provided a plan for His people to rest and recover *during* their working lives. As best I can determine, God has not prescribed a time when we should retire. We have arbitrarily decided that at age 62, 65, or some later period, our active working careers should stop. Nothing could be further from the truth, and we should begin to adjust to a saner and more reasonable philosophy.

Storing some funds during the most productive years of your life for the later years is both logical and biblical. As Proverbs 6:6 says, *"Go to the ant, O sluggard, observe her ways and be wise, which, having no chief, officer or ruler, prepares her food in the summer, and gathers her provision in the harvest."* Having some reserve allows you to take more frequent sabbaticals later in life or to volunteer your services to ministries without the necessity of being paid. But if you want to live the long, happy life that God has prescribed for you, don't retire![31]

What a great history lesson on retirement that Larry provides as well as great insight into God's prescribed method of rest and relaxation, namely a sabbatical.

I don't want to condemn anyone for how they're living out their later years. I would, however, like to build on what Larry Burkett wrote in his book and talk about the good as well as the bad aspects of the way we think about retirement today.

Earning and Saving While You're Able (a good thing)

One very admirable motivation for saving for retirement is to take the approach that it's important to save money while you're more physically and mentally able to earn money (when you're younger) so that when you're not as physically and mentally able to earn money (when you're older), you'll be able to live off of your savings.

Is there anything wrong with that train of thought? My quick answer is no. It sounds like common sense and a prudent and responsible way to manage one's abilities and one's money.

America's rate of savings, for individuals as well as for our government, has for many years been low, nonexistent, or even negative (meaning we're spending more than we're earning). This does not bode well for individuals, nor for the country as a whole, particularly as the ability of social security to pay for even basic costs of living in future years for an aging population seems less reliable every year.

"A good man leaves an inheritance to his children's children" (Proverbs 13:22 NKJV). This certainly speaks highly of the discipline of saving one's money.

When it comes to prosperity, too many people in America, including some Christians, are too focused on their own personal prosperity and not on *posterity*, namely the prosperity of future generations.

If all we're doing is trying to be prosperous so we can enjoy ourselves, either now or in retirement, without any thought to leaving something for our children, our church, or some other ministry to further God's Kingdom, I view that as selfish and outside of God's will.

We've already said it's a good thing to work and earn money. We've also said it's good to tithe and to give. I would add to that list of desirable habits that of saving. We should save so we can take care of ourselves financially in the future as well as provide for future generations.

It's also worth noting that in some cases, due to health reasons or just the nature of one's work, a person is basically forced to retire at a certain age, so it's prudent to save now.

Giving Back as a Volunteer
(another good thing)

There are countless organizations, good organizations, that are helping others and/or advancing the Kingdom of God, that rely heavily on the contributions of volunteers, many of whom are retirees.

My parents are both retired and are active volunteers. They get a lot of satisfaction from their volunteer time and they're certainly blessing a lot of people in the process.

In the Chapter *You're Already a Missionary*, I made the point that we shouldn't make the mistake of thinking that we can't serve God if our job is not what most people would consider *full-time ministry*.

That same logic applies as well to our retirement as it does to what most would call our *working years*. We can all live out God's purpose for our work (to love Him) as well as His assignment for our work, in every phase of our lives, including retirement, even if we're not doing *full-time ministry*.

You might say there's an attitude of *service* that goes along with volunteering that we should all aspire to our entire lives. You can have the attitude of a volunteer even if you're getting paid for your job.

As my friend Dr. Griffin says, "should not a time come when all one's work is volunteer?"

Don't Think of Work as a Necessary Evil

As we've discussed, you can't have a divine purpose for your work if your purpose is simply to acquire money for yourself. That's true if you're going to use your money simply to indulge yourself in the here and now. It can also be true if you're going to save for your retirement, particularly if your focus is on a retirement that's all about you.

I think we can all make the mistake of being too focused on our retirement, painting a picture in our mind, a fantasy, that retirement will be so much better than our working life is now.

By doing so, we invest ourselves, our energy and our emotions, in an uncertain and unrealistic future and in so doing miss out on all that God has for us right here, right now, in our work and at our job every day.

By thinking of our retirement as being drastically different than our working years, we may end up planning for and living out a retirement that is primarily made up of leisurely activities without any spiritual substance.

Am I saying it's a sin to slow down and play a lot of golf when you retire? No. I do think, however, that Larry Burkett was onto something in his book when he suggested that God's way of resting was to take an occasional sabbatical rather than a permanent vacation.

Plan for a Commencement,
Not a Finish Line

Finish line is defined as "A line that marks the end of a course for racing."[32] One definition of *commencement* is "an act or instance of commencing; beginning"[33].

If you think of your life and your work as a race where the primary goal is to finish, I don't think you'll appreciate the journey along the way, as you should.

As my friend Dr. Griffin pointed out, graduations are called commencements because they're the beginning of a new phase in life.

I think that's a great way to think about retirement. It's the beginning of a new phase in your life, in a similar way, perhaps, to the way we should think of our *heavenly retirement*. We're not going to be spending all of eternity playing a harp while floating on a cloud any more, I believe, than we should be idling down our lives to a standstill when we retire.

When you get right down to it, I guess my thoughts on retirement are very similar to my thoughts on how we should think of our daily work. Our focus should be on the here and now and our focus should be on God and not on ourselves.

So here are some closing thoughts on retirement:

- Go ahead and save your money so that you won't have to rely on the government or others to pay for your living expenses in case you're not able to earn money in your later years.

- Stop thinking of your work as a necessary evil and start thinking of it as the divine and wonderful privilege that God has provided for you.

- Stop focusing on your retirement so much and start focusing on today and on what God wants you to do at your work and in your life here and now.

- Stop thinking of leisure and idleness as an ideal way to spend your time. That's true whether you're thinking of now (how you spend your nights and your weekends) or whether you're thinking of your future. Instead, think about all the ways you can find joy and purpose in being active and productive, using your desires, your skills, and your talents to help others and to be a part of God's greater plan.

- Eliminate the concept of *finish line* from your thinking with regard to your work and your life. Enjoy and be purposeful about your journey today and leave tomorrow to God.

So far in our journey together, we've discussed the extent of the problem when we lack a divine purpose for our work. We've talked about dreaming with purpose by understanding our true divine purpose and assignment for our work.

We've also begun the process of renewing our mind by taking a peek at the heart of Jesus when it comes to work and work-related topics. We want to finish the last part of our journey by reflecting on an important verse from the book of James: that encourages us to take action.

PART 4

Act Like Jesus

But be doers of the word, and not hearers only, deceiving yourselves. For if anyone is a hearer of the word and not a doer, he is like a man observing his natural face in a mirror; for he observes himself, goes away, and immediately forgets what kind of man he was. But he who looks into the perfect law of liberty and continues *in it,* and is not a forgetful hearer but a doer of the work, this one will be blessed in what he does.

—James 1:22-25 (NKJV)

Be Great at What You Do

Whatever you do, do all to the glory of God.

—1 Corinthians 10:31 (NKJV)

If we have a divine purpose of loving God at our work and we've begun to think like Jesus by renewing our mind through His Word, the next step is to be a doer of the Word and to act like Jesus.

In the remainder of this book, we're going to discuss four divine work assignments. I call them *general* divine work assignments since I believe that God gave them to all of us.

Earlier in the book we talked about how to find your *personal* divine work assignment, the perfect job that God has planned just for you. While I may not know exactly what God's unique, personal assignment is for your work or your career and I can only give you suggestions on how to find it, I do know with certainty that He's given each and every one of us, including you, some very clear and specific direction when it comes to our work.

You might say that your personal divine work assignment is *what* you do, and your general work assignment is *how* you do it.

In this last part of the book, we're going to talk about how you do your work.

The first assignment we're going to discuss, "Be Great at What You Do," is probably best expressed by King Solomon. Solomon commanded us, "Whatever your hand finds to do, do *it* with your might;" (Ecclesiastes 9:10 NKJV).

The How is Greater than the What

By using the word *whatever* in the first part of his statement, Solomon showed he wasn't too concerned about our job title or what type of work we do, but rather on how we do the work that we do.

I think this is an important point. Just as we can have a divine purpose (loving God) regardless of the type of work we do, we can also have a divine assignment (in this case, being great at what we do) regardless of the type of work we do.

I think we need to add some kind of caveat here. If the type of work we do brings us in direct conflict with what we know from God's Word to be His heart, His ways, and His commands, I don't think that kind of work counts as a *whatever*. Being a drug dealer or prostitute comes to mind.

Two Ways to be Great

It's interesting what Solomon focuses on in the second part of his statement "do *it* with your might."

There are at least two main ways we can be great, or practice excellence, with the work that we do.

First, we can be very skilled in our work. We all know people who are able to do their job well without seeming to work too hard. This may be because they have a natural ability to do the job they do, or it may be the result of them developing their skill over a long period of time. Through repetition and consistency, they've taken what used to be a challenge for them and made it routine and predictable.

But there's a second way we can be great at what we do, and that is not through skill but rather through our sheer effort. Call it what you want: grit, hutzpah, oomph, hard work, spunk, or tenacity. Those people who have achieved the highest levels in their work, those who are honored and revered by their peers and others, typically have a combination of natural ability *and* hard work.

Famous people like Albert Einstein and Michael Jordan come to mind. Their natural abilities gave them an advantage with their careers, and by applying hard work they were able to achieve things that would otherwise not have been possible.

It's this second way of being great, though—working hard—to which Solomon is specifically referring when he says "do *it* with your might." It's also something which we can all do in our work, without exception. Regardless of our natural ability or how much experience we have in a job or task, we can all do our work with our might, and we can do it starting today. When we dedicate ourselves to working hard at our job and doing the best we can, I believe we are great at what we do in the eyes of Jesus, regardless how we are recognized by others.

Hard Work as a Testimony

If we're working hard for the right reason, as a loving response to God and not an attempt to impress our boss or our coworkers, our hard work can be a powerful testimony to others.

If you pour yourself into your work and do your job to the best of your ability, your coworkers will be impressed and inspired, and probably even more so than by someone who doesn't work that hard but has natural abilities.

If, at the same time, you make it known that you're a Christian, they'll be impressed not just with you, but more importantly by what God is doing *through* you and how He has changed you for the better. On the other hand, if as a professed Christian you're lazy, just doing the bare minimum to get through the day and keep from getting fired, you'll send a very different signal to those with whom you work about what the Christian life is all about.

If you asked my coworkers if I was a Christian, most would probably say yes for no other reason than I'm pretty open with my faith, and hopefully also by the way I act and treat others. If you asked my coworkers to describe me either as someone with natural abilities or a hard worker, they would probably call me a hard worker.

Keep the Right Focus

Because working hard is something that requires action on our part, there's always a temptation to take credit for our hard work and in the process focus on ourselves and not on God. That's probably more of a temptation here in America than anywhere else, where self-reliance is so highly valued. God is the one and only source for both our talent as well as our effort, and without Him we wouldn't be able to do any work at all, let alone do it well.

Earlier, we referred to the story of Joseph as an example of being faithful and trusting God with the bigger picture. It's worth noting that while Joseph was being faithful, God was working through Joseph to reveal Himself through the excellent work Joseph was performing.

After Joseph was sold by his brothers as a slave, he was then sold to Potiphar, the captain of the guard for Pharaoh in Egypt. Not long after that, Potiphar recognized that the Lord was with Joseph and that God gave Joseph success. As a result, Potiphar put Joseph in charge of his entire household.

Later, after Joseph was imprisoned after being falsely accused, Pharaoh recognized Joseph's discerning and wisdom that had come from God by making him second in command for all of Egypt. Potiphar and Pharaoh both promoted Joseph, but they also recognized it was God who was responsible for Joseph's excellent work.

Paul said "whatever you do, do all to the glory of God." (1 Corinthians 10:31 NKJV). Any of our hard work should be to His glory, not ours.

Normal Christian Behavior

"I beseech you therefore, brethren, by the mercies of God, that you present your bodies a living sacrifice, holy, acceptable to God, *which is* your reasonable service." (Romans 12:1 NKJV).

Hard work is one way to live out this verse. Note that making ourselves a living sacrifice is not something out of the ordinary or exceptional on our part, it's our *reasonable service*. Or as one of my favorite pastors was apt to say, "that's just *normal* behavior for a Christian."[34]

In those verses just mentioned in 1 Corinthians and Romans, Paul doesn't speak specifically about work, but I believe this refers to every aspect of our lives. I'm including them here partly because I believe that one key to finding peace and purpose in life is to be fully integrated, to be the same person at home, at work, and at play.

As a result, just about anything the Bible has to say about living our lives in general applies as well to our workplace as it does to every other part of our life. Having said that, it's worth noting that Paul also had some very specific things to say about work.

> Slaves, obey your earthly masters with deep respect and fear. Serve them sincerely as you would serve Christ. Try to please them all the time, not just when they are watching you. As slaves of Christ, do the will of God with all your heart. Work with enthusiasm, as though you were working for the Lord rather than for people. Remember that the Lord will reward each one of us for the good we do, whether we are slaves or free.
>
> Ephesians 6:5–8 (New Living Translation)

If we truly embrace the idea that we are serving *Christ* through our work, it should change our whole attitude about our work, for the better. As a result, we will naturally work harder and do a much better job, which will naturally lead to earthly as well as heavenly rewards.

We should also find more purpose and satisfaction in the work we do. It's important to absorb these verses and fully grasp the real reason why you should want to excel at your work. After all, the fact that being great at what you do is a good idea is something you can find in just about any secular book on success or self-help. The reasons, however, for seeking excellence in your work, will vary widely depending on what worldview the author is coming from.

We should not try to be our best at work because we want to impress our boss, get a promotion, make more money, get ahead, because we want our company to succeed, because of a general desire for excellence, or because of a desire to prove something to ourselves. We also shouldn't come up with a *spiritual* reason for hard work that is detached from Jesus Christ. We shouldn't work hard in order to create good karma or cooperate with a mystical law of the universe.

We should work hard for one reason—because we love God.

Working hard, after all, is really just another form of worship, another way of expressing our love for Him. The really great news is that by seeking God rather than seeking a promotion, we'll get the promotion too!

One of the best compliments I ever got from one of my bosses during one of my performance reviews was that he respected the work that I did and how I did it. I think he was referring to my hard work ethic, but beyond that I'd like to think he was recognizing my integrity in how I went about my job in general. To me, hard work is just one of many ways to show integrity when you're at work.

We're going to expand on this idea of integrity in the workplace in the next chapter.

Model Integrity

"If you sign here, I can leave you connected; otherwise I need to cut you off."

—Service technician from the gas company, name unknown

There was an awkward silence as the words of the technician echoed in our ears. I stared at the paperwork on the clipboard in front of me as several of our maintenance techs looked at me, waiting for my response.

The day had started out pretty uneventful. As the facilities engineer, I was responsible for managing several different projects for the relatively small organization for whom I worked.

Midway through the morning, on the way to check on the progress of a new chiller installation for our heating and air system on the north end of the complex, I caught a whiff of gas. I stopped to investigate. There was a gas meter nearby, but I couldn't tell exactly where the smell was coming from.

About an hour later, after a phone call to our natural gas provider, a service rep pulled up in his pick-up truck to check things out. He unlocked one of his toolboxes, pulled out a detection device, and began to take readings around that end of the building.

After about ten minutes, a bit frustrated, he said he couldn't find the source of the leak. He went on to explain that his company required him to turn off the gas in this situation, unless we would sign the form he was holding in front of me.

I glanced around to several of our maintenance techs who had joined the conversation, then I read just above the signature line on the form. It basically said that we had identified the source of the gas leak and corrected it.

"I don't want to shut you down," the man said. "This is a pretty common thing. I've done what I can do for now, you can keep looking for the source and correct it, but I have to get going."

I knew what was at stake. Our production and our ability to make money depended on this gas line. If he shut us off, all the testing for the day would be wasted and the materials our client had paid for along with the results they were expecting would be worthless. This could be costly.

The temptation to sign on the dotted line was strong. The only problem was that he was asking me to lie, and I wasn't going to do it.

Once I refused to sign the paper, everyone jumped into action.

We grabbed some shovels, brainstormed on the most likely place to find the leak, and started digging. The service rep stuck around for another half hour while we dug and searched. Finally, we unearthed a valve with a questionable-looking connection. The service rep held his detector next to the valve and confirmed that was the source of the leak.

Fortunately, we were able to isolate the valve and replace it without shutting gas off to the whole facility. The smell was gone, the gas company rep drove off, and everyone went back to work.

Webster defines integrity to be "the quality of being honest and fair" It also equates the word integrity to "incorruptibility"[35].

We can all think of ways integrity can be demonstrated in the workplace. Here are some that come to my mind.

Be Honest

Having high integrity means being honest at work, all the time, even when it's not convenient.

I know based on comments made to me later that day that I irritated several people that day, including someone at the top of our organization. They apparently felt that my refusal to sign the form was irresponsible.

But if I had gone along with the suggestion of the person from the gas company, I'm confident we probably would not have placed the same importance on finding that leak as we did once we knew there was a threat of our gas being turned off. Who knows what could have happened?

God honored my decision by providing a solution. The leak was found and our gas stayed on, and we were able to continue to operate safely. But I didn't have to think through the possible consequences of the gas leak going unfound. It was enough to know that signing that form was a lie and that God told me not to lie.

Being honest also includes fessing up when you've made a mistake, even when no one knows about it. It's always better to admit your mistake and face the consequences than to try and cover it up or hope no one notices.

If you're dealing with someone either inside or outside of your company on a business matter, tell the whole truth to whomever you're dealing with and don't withhold important information because you think it would weaken your position. Dishonesty by omission is just as bad as dishonesty by commission.

Don't Play Favorites

Hopefully, you work for an organization that has rules of ethics that are enforced that guard against someone getting preferential treatment. Whether they do or not, it's best to look to God's Word for your standard.

"You shall not pervert justice; you shall not show partiality, nor take a bribe, for a bribe blinds the eyes of the wise and twists the words of the righteous." (Deuteronomy 16:19 NKJV).

The pharisees recognized the integrity of Jesus when they sent their disciples to Him-"'Teacher,' they said, 'we know how honest you are. You teach the way of God truthfully. You are impartial and don't play favorites.'" (Matthew 22:16 NLT).

Paul reminds us in his letter to the Ephesians that God is impartial:

"And you, masters, do the same things to them, giving up threatening, knowing that your own Master also is in heaven, and there is no partiality with Him." (Ephesians 6:9 NKJV).

As an engineer, I have dealt a lot with sales people and contractors who are seeking business with the company for whom I work. Sometimes they will want to bring free donuts, buy me lunch, take me golfing, or give me sports tickets.

While this can be important as part of relationship building, there is a danger this will affect my judgment, and as a result I have chosen to limit accepting gifts such as these as much as possible.

Sometimes it's not a matter of whether or not you accept a gift but rather the size of the gift. You should certainly follow your company's rules in this area, but if your conscience holds you to a higher standard, go with the Holy Spirit. You may want to limit receipt of a gift only to those with whom you're already doing business as opposed to someone seeking to do business with you or your company. I've found that when I consistently hold myself to a high standard in this area, I stop getting gift offers from those I work with consistently which makes the decision making process for me that much easier.

Recently I was particularly tempted in this area of partiality. I was speaking with one of the salesmen I deal with about a mission trip he had gone on with his wife and I was similarly sharing about our fundraising efforts for a mission trip my oldest daughter was going on to Africa.

He told me that his wife owned a clothing store and he offered to dedicate one evening's receipts from their store toward my daughter's mission trip. My first thought was *Hey, that sounds great*. After thinking about it further,

I realized that just because he was a Christian offering to help a "Christian cause" shouldn't change the standard I was trying to hold to when it came to favoritism and partiality at work.

Another area where partiality comes into play is how you treat others you work with. You should not let your personal feelings about other employees affect your treatment of them. If someone rubs you the wrong way, you should give them the same professional courtesy with your work as those with whom you consider to be your friends.

Don't Gossip

"Avoid worthless, foolish talk that only leads to more godless behavior." (2 Timothy 2:16 NLT)

"You shall not bear false witness against your neighbor." (Exodus 20:16 NKJV).

Don't ever participate in gossip.

After running my own business for many years and returning to the workplace, I was amazed and disappointed how common gossip was where I worked.

Gossip can be extremely damaging to individuals as well as to the organization as a whole. I've heard Dave Ramsey, a nationally known radio show host and teacher, talk about how gossip is cause for immediate termination at his company

Fortunately for his employees, Dave recognizes what a destructive practice gossip can be. Whether or not you have that kind of commitment from the leaders of your organization, you can hold a high standard for yourself.

There are several ways you can live this out at work, each one being more difficult but more valuable than the next.

1. **Don't Join In**–you can simply refuse to join in a conversation when someone begins to speak negatively about someone else at work or begins to share something that should not be shared.

2. **Walk Away**–A better thing to do than to simply refuse to participate is to walk away when you hear someone gossiping, even if it might seem awkward or rude to do so. After all, they are the ones who should feel awkward, not you.

3. **Confront It**–The best thing to do, though, is to confront the gossip by letting the gossiper know that you don't appreciate it and by reminding them of the harm it does to the victim of the gossip as well as to the whole organization. It's not easy to do this and you'll no doubt ruffle some feathers, especially if you confront the gossiper; but when you've got a divine purpose and assignment at work, you just can't help yourself!

Don't Use Foul Language or Tell Off-Color Jokes

"Obscene stories, foolish talk, and coarse jokes—these are not for you. Instead, let there be thankfulness to God." (Ephesians 5:4 NLT).

In the place I worked after returning to the workplace, nearly everyone cursed on a regular basis, and some of the workers regularly told off-color jokes.

Most of them tried to censor themselves (though not always) when I was around since they knew I didn't appreciate it. Just as with gossip, I addressed this by refusing to participate, by walking away from inappropriate conversations, even if they were with my boss, and sometimes by confronting it directly.

One time, I asked my boss to have pornography removed from the bathrooms at work. That made me a target for the guys who liked to have those magazines in those stalls, but it also was an excellent opportunity for me to be a role model for what was right.

Don't Lose Your Temper

"People with understanding control their anger; a hot temper shows great foolishness" (Proverbs 14:29 NLT).

"So then, my beloved brethren, let every man be swift to hear, slow to speak, slow to wrath;" (James 1:19 NKJV)

There is no place for anger in the workplace, and those who express anger, even if only on an occasional basis, contribute to an unhealthy and unsafe work environment. You'll stand out like a beacon of light and be looked at as a stable, steady, peaceful, and reliable coworker when you exercise the discipline required to never lose your temper at work, especially if you work somewhere where others do lose their temper.

Don't Envy

"A sound heart *is* life to the body, But envy *is* rottenness to the bones." (Proverbs 14:30 NKJV).

It's embarrassing to admit, but I struggle with this issue. I'd love to say that I'm always happy for the success of my coworkers and that I don't compare myself to others at work, including their title, how well they do their work, and how much money they make.

I'd love to say that it's enough for me to simply appreciate my own job and all the blessings that come with it and that I sincerely want others around me to succeed and prosper just as much as I want that for myself.

I'd love to say all those things but it wouldn't be true.

The extent to which I give in to envy I open the door for the devil to steal from me my joy and purpose while I'm at work in a big way.

What can I say, I'm a work in progress.

Don't Be Judgmental

"Judge not, that you be not judged." (Matthew 7:1 NKJV)

As harmful as being envious is to the joy and purpose that God wants for you to have in your work, I think that having a judgmental spirit may be even worse.

Just as with envy, this falls under the "do as I say and not as I do" category.

I have often kept score, so to speak, of how others do their work, including the hours they keep and whether they approach their work with the same standards that I believe I do.

When I do this, I'm living like a Pharisee and I'm bound by a works mentality.

I believe that Jesus taught that the condition of our heart is more important than the works of our hands, and that neglecting the former in favor of the latter is not pleasing to Him and not good for us.

If you struggle with envy and judgment at work as I do, I hope that my honesty has given you someone to whom you can relate and that it may provide you with some comfort. At the same time, I pray that you'll join me in the full realization of how harmful these conditions of the heart can be to ourselves. Please also join me as I continue to seek God's will in these areas and let God take over, that He would be weak when I'm strong.

My pastor once said that refusing to forgive is like drinking poison and hoping that the other person dies[36].

I think the same is true for envy and judgment as it is for refusing to forgive. When we envy or judge our coworkers, we may hurt others but the primary victim is ourselves. You can open the door to God's blessings for your work by believing on His promises and understanding and living by His ways, but you can just as quickly shut that door if you give in to the devil and listen to his whispering lies about your coworkers having a better job than you, or judging them because they're not doing their job the way you think they should.

Don't settle for this "occupational hazard"!

Why Is Modeling Integrity So Important?

The Bible describes a number of benefits that come as a result of modeling integrity.

"He who walks with integrity walks securely, But he who perverts his ways will become known." (Proverbs 10:9 NKJV).

"For You, O LORD, will bless the righteous; With favor You will surround him as *with* a shield." (Psalm 5:12 NKJV).

Just imagine yourself spending your entire day at work being surrounded with a shield of favor by the Creator and Ruler of the universe. I have not only imagined that but experienced it in very tangible ways, and I highly recommend it.

Another huge benefit of modeling integrity at your work is the positive impact it will have on others with whom you work.

If you have children, then you know how big of an impact you have on them. They are constantly watching you to see how you respond to various situations in life as well as looking to see what kind of values you stand for.

Now draw a parallel from the natural to the spiritual. Whether they realize it or not, those who are babies spiritually are constantly watching those who are more mature spiritually. You may not think of yourself as particularly spiritually mature, but there are many people who work with you who are not attending church, who are not spending time in God's Word, who are not saved, and for whom you may be their most significant spiritual role model. What you say and what you do matters in every aspect of your life, but it's particularly important where you work because of the amount of time you spend there and the number of people you affect.

In the same way that your children have no choice but to hang around with you a lot (you may have heard it said, "you can choose your friends, but you can't choose your family"), your coworkers are essentially forced to spend a lot of their time around their coworkers, including you.

Please know that what you say at work matters, but what you *do* matters even more. Ralph Waldo Emerson said it well: "What you do speaks so loudly that I cannot hear what you say."[37]. You don't have to go around preaching to others at work in order to influence others in a positive way. When it comes to modeling integrity, your actions will speak volumes and will be much more effective than anything you could ever say to them about integrity.

In addition to being great at what you do and being a model of integrity, you can also take action and live out God's assignment for your work by loving and serving your coworkers.

We'll talk about this wonderful assignment in the next chapter.

Love and Serve Others

"By this all will know that you are My disciples, if you have love for one another."

—Jesus of Nazareth speaking in
John 13:35, NKJV

I looked at my phone to see who was calling. It was the secretary at the front desk.

"You have some boxes of gifts up front," she said as I picked up the phone.

"Let me guess," I said, as she then finished my sentence for me.

We both knew who the gifts were from because it was Valentine's Day. The same person dropped off gifts at work for me, my wife, and all three of my daughters this day every year, as well as on every Halloween, Christmas, and Easter.

This person, I'll call her Shelly, used to work in the quality laboratory where I first came to work in 2009. She was a contract worker and didn't have the same benefits as the employees in the lab. She didn't make a lot of money, and when she started having some serious health issues, she was concerned about being able to pay her rent one month. I knew this because she and I talked on a regular basis about our lives outside of work and about our love for Jesus.

Fortunately, God had blessed my wife and I financially, and we had been setting aside money in our budget each month so we would always be able to give when we felt led to do so.

When I told my wife about Shelly's situation, we both came to the same conclusion quickly. We mailed her a check for the amount of her rent.

Not too long after that, Shelly had to quit her job due to health problems. Her situation eventually improved, and one day we received a check from her to repay us for our gift. Shelly and I didn't communicate much after that, but starting with the next holiday, the gifts started showing up at work.

And when I say "gifts" with an *s* on the end, I mean *gifts*. I typically have to make more than one trip to the car to carry them all.

We've developed a ritual where I show the gifts to my family when I get home, I call Shelly; and using the speaker phone feature on my cell phone, we all yell thanking her and telling her we love her. I suppose she's being blessed over and over in the same way we are.

Love God First

Though this shouldn't be our motivation for loving and serving, I must say that when I have loved and served others at work, I've generally received something in return, either something very tangible, as with Shelly, or just a feeling of satisfaction.

Having said that, I must admit that this assignment is definitely not one that comes naturally to me. I've often heard other Christians referred to as having a *servant's heart*. I don't think of myself that way, and I typically have to step out of my comfort zone to love or serve. I also have found that if I'm not loving and serving God first, I'm very unlikely to love and serve others.

During His ministry, Jesus was asked the most important commandment of all. He responded:

> "'You shall love the Lord your God with all your heart, with all your soul, and with all your mind.' This is *the* first and great commandment. And *the* second *is* like it: 'You shall love your neighbor as yourself.'
>
> Matthew 22:37-39 (NKJV)

The reason He listed those two commandments in that order may be that you can't truly love and serve others without first loving and seeking God. That must have been part of the plan when God gave Moses the Ten Commandments (see Exodus 20:3–17, Deuteronomy 5:7–21). Commandments 1–4 all deal with our relationship with God, while commandments 5–10 deal with our relationship with others.

Be a Positive Force

"So encourage each other and build each other up, just as you are already doing." (1 Thessalonians 5:11 NLT).

Every day at work you have an opportunity to either be a positive or negative force for those with whom you work.

If you have a divine purpose at work and love God, you will naturally want to be a positive force and let the love of God flow through you to others. Like me, you probably regularly ask people you work with how they're doing. It's easy to do and it fills a potentially awkward silent moment when you're passing them in the hall. With a divine purpose, it will be hard for you to just brush it off when someone gives you an answer that let's you know something is wrong.

When you start really caring and asking your coworkers what's wrong in those situations and start doing more listening than talking, God will present you with incredible opportunities to show His love for others.

Seize the Moment

If someone seems to be having a bad day, take time to find out why they're having a bad day, listen to them, and offer them words of encouragement. You may also want to ask them if they would mind if you prayed for them. You can pray for them later in your private prayer time, but I think it's even better if you can pray *with* them right there on the spot.

I was nervous the first time I asked one of my coworkers if they would let me pray with them. I soon found out that no one ever refused me.

Praying for and with my coworkers, out loud but in private, with my hand on their shoulder, has been one of the most satisfying things I've ever done at work. This should be done discreetly out of respect for the other person and so as not to interrupt the other business going on around you.

There are a number of great things that can happen as a result of praying with someone.

1. Connection–You can *both* connect with *God* as you pray in agreement, but you can also connect with your *coworker* in a way that may not have been possible any other way. If you're like me, you'll remember what their struggle was and do a much better job of following up and asking them about it if you pray with them rather than just listen to what they have to say.

2. Remembrance–It may sound like a simple thing and most relevant for someone starting in a new job, but you may find that by praying for and caring for your fellow employees, you'll more easily remember their names.

3. Much More… Prayers are answered, burdens removed, God moves, and good things happen (see Matthew 18:19). I can personally testify to all of these benefits.

Be a Lighthouse in the Storm

"Share each other's burdens, and in this way obey the law of Christ." (Galatians 6:2 NLT).

"And be kind to one another, tenderhearted, forgiving one another, even as God in Christ forgave you." (Ephesians 4:32 NKJV).

God wants us to help each other. Many of your coworkers carry burdens from their personal lives that, for whatever reason, they're not able or willing to share with others.

If you have a divine purpose at your work, you'll find that your coworkers will look to you to share their burdens because they'll recognize you as a safe, reliable, and trustworthy person. They'll see Jesus *in* you and be drawn to Him *through* you.

What a privilege to have someone confide in you. Don't squander that opportunity!

Love Your Enemy

"If your enemy is hungry, give him bread to eat; And if he is thirsty, give him water to drink; For *so* you will heap coals of fire on his head, And the Lord will reward you" (Proverbs 25:21-22 NKJV).

A great way to show God's love at work is to show it toward those with whom you would normally consider your enemies; a more gentle way of saying enemies might be those who don't seem to be on your side.

You know who I'm talking about:

1. The guy who gives you the hardest time when you make a mistake and never wants to let it go.
2. The executive who ignores your existence and never bothers to remember your name.
3. The secretary who is the gossip queen and who has betrayed your trust by sharing something you said to her in private.

Jesus said, "For if you love those who love you, what reward have you? Do not even the tax collectors do the same?" (Matthew 5:46 NKJV).

Time and time again, Jesus loved the unlovable, and He calls us to do the same.

Be a Servant Leader

Whether or not you have people reporting to you at work or have the title *manager* on your business card or office door, you're a leader. We're all leaders.

There's been a lot of talk, in secular as well as faith-based books, that being a servant leader is the most effective way to lead. Jesus knew this truth long ago, and He gave the perfect example as the servant leader.

When He met with His disciples on the night in which He was betrayed, He washed their feet.

"If I then, your Lord and Master, have washed your feet; ye also ought to wash one another's feet. For I have given you an example, that ye should do as I have done to you." (John 13:14-15 KJV).

Regardless of your position or title at work, start to think of yourself as a servant—a servant to your boss and to your company, of course but also a servant—to each and every employee you work with as well as to clients, vendors, and others outside of your organization you interact with.

"Live in harmony with each other. Don't be too proud to enjoy the company of ordinary people. And don't think you know it all!" (Romans 12:16 NLT).

We can love and serve others by simply listening and responding to their needs. Perhaps the greatest way to love others, though, is to share with them the greatest gift of all, Jesus Christ, and to help them grow and mature in their relationship with Christ.

We'll talk about that awesome assignment from God in the next chapter.

Share the Good News
and Make Disciples

And He said to them, "Go into all the world and
preach the gospel to every creature.

—Mark 16:15 (NKJV)

Go therefore and make disciples of all the nations,
baptizing them in the name of the Father and of
the Son and of the Holy Spirit.

—Matthew 28:19 (NKJV)

I looked over at the door from my booth in Burger
King, then up at the clock, probably for the fifth time
since I arrived. It was 12:39 p.m. No one appeared to be
coming today. I wasn't surprised, but I was a bit frustrated
and disappointed.

Seven weeks earlier, I posted a sign at the bulletin
board at work by the time clock where everyone passed
by twice a day. I also sent out an e-mail with the same
announcement, that I was doing a study over lunch at the
nearby Burger King, going through one of my favorite
books *A Better Way to Pray*[38].

I was recently born again at the time and fired up about living my life differently, about living for Jesus, though I was still trying to figure out what that meant, particularly in the workplace.

One week after posting my sign, I drove the mile or so over to Burger King, slipped into a booth with my lunch and waited, armed with my book, my Bible, and some thoughts on what I would say if someone were to show up.

I decided after that first no-show day that I would use my lunch hour each week to do my own study and that I wouldn't get annoyed or take it personally if no one showed up. I did a pretty good job with the first part, not so well with the second.

What were they afraid of? I wondered. *Weren't they just a little curious what the book was about? What was keeping them away? Were they concerned about what others would think? Did they just not like me?*

No one ever did show up for the study, and I don't know that I ever got adequate answers to my questions, but I continued trying different things to bring awareness of Jesus and His message into my job each day.

A Simple Way to Know You're in His Will

If you ever find yourself wondering if you're in God's will, all you have to do is share the Gospel.

I first heard that concept from someone I just met while we were test driving his pickup just before buying it from him[39]. I couldn't agree with him more.

Testifying to the truth and sharing the Gospel was an integral part of Jesus' ministry and actually His stated reason for coming into the world (see John 18:37).

"And He said to them, "Go into all the world and preach the gospel to every creature." (Mark 16:15 NKJV)

This command from our Savior, often referred to as the "Great Commission," did not come with any conditions or exceptions. He didn't say this was to be done for only the Greeks or the Jews, or to be done only by the missionaries, full-time pastors, or others considered by men to be adequately "trained."

He also didn't say we should only do this as part of a church evangelism outing or only when we're *not* at our jobs.

It's always a good idea to share the good news of the Gospel, *always*. Now there *is* a difference between sharing the Gospel and making disciples. We'll talk about that distinction later in this chapter.

Hell Is Real

If you truly believe that heaven and hell are real places, and if you consider loving God to be your divine work purpose, then out of compassion for your fellow coworkers you will want to save them from hell at any cost.

I think one of the most compelling arguments I've seen for sharing the Gospel ironically came from a nonbeliever in the form of a letter sent to Ray Comfort and posted on the website for the evangelism ministry *Way of the Master*[40]:

Ray,

You are really convinced that you've got all the answers. You've really got yourself tricked into believing that you're 100% right. Well, let me tell you just one thing. Do you consider yourself to be compassionate of other humans? If you're right, as you say you are, and believe that, then how can you sleep at night? When you speak with me you are speaking with someone who you believe is walking directly into eternal damnation into an endless onslaught of horrendous pain which your 'loving' god created, yet you stand by and do nothing.

If you believe one bit that thousands every day were falling into an eternal and unreacheable fate, you should be running the streets mad with rage at their blindness. That's equivalent to standing on a street corner and watching every person that passes you walk blindly directly into the path of a bus and die, yet you stand idly by and do nothing. You're just twiddling your thumbs, happy in the knowledge that one day that 'walk' signal will shine your way across the road.

Think about it. Imagine the horrors Hell must have in store if the bible is true. You're just going to allow that to happen and not care about saving anyone but yourself? If you're right then you're an uncaring, unemotional and purely selfish (expletive) that has no right to talk about subjects such as love and caring.

I've heard it said that the best way to think of unbelievers we come across is not as our enemies, but as captives in chains, bound up by the lies and deceptions of the devil[41]. I think that's a good suggestion. I also think the atheist who wrote to Ray Comfort, and his arguably justified anger toward Christians who don't evangelize, may be a helpful reminder for us when we're out and about at work around unbelievers.

How You Share Matters

The apostle Paul encouraged us to exercise care when talking with others about our faith.

> Live wisely among those who are not believers, and make the most of every opportunity. Let your conversation be gracious and attractive so that you will have the right response for everyone.
>
> Colossians 4:5-6 (NLT)

How we share the good news can be just as important as whether or not we choose to do it. Our gracious and attractive manner can have a huge impact on how the person receives *our* message as well as how they receive from other Christians. Remember, you may just be preparing someone's heart for the next person who shares with them the Gospel.

An easy way to start sharing the Gospel at work is simply to invite others to your church. If you're not in a church that unashamedly speaks the whole truth from the Bible, then please find one!

If you *are* in that kind of church, tell others at your work about it. The ideal situation is to wait until the person brings up something related to church, essentially opening the door for you to enter.

If that doesn't happen, though, you can just wait until you feel prompted by the Holy Spirit and then ask the person if they're at a church they like. This is a simple way to transition the conversation from the natural, or small talk, to the spiritual. By asking that simple question, you're in effect making it safe for them to talk about spiritual things.

If they say no, invite them to your church. Try to always have a stack of business cards from your church handy. It's easy to hand someone a card and just let them know that your church has been a blessing to you. You can jot down on the card an inspiring Bible verse or a website where they can grow with some good teaching.

If they say yes, that they're in a good church, use it as an opportunity to ask them more about their faith and to share with them about yours. You can help build up their faith as well as yours by sharing with them details about your walk with God. Tell them about events you're attending at your church or about a spiritual truth that has recently made an impact on you.

Always be open to what the Holy Spirit prompts you to say in these situations while at the same time having a plan ahead of time about what you're going to say. There are a lot of great evangelism resources out there to get you started including the website *Way of the Master* led by Ray Comfort and Kirk Cameron[42].

T-Shirts and Other Billboards

There are a lot of ways to share the good news that don't involve moving your lips. Someone who once worked as a contract custodian where I worked never talked about his faith, but he wore t-shirts every day that boldly proclaimed his Christian beliefs. This was encouraging to me, and I told him so.

I had guessed that his shirts were encouraging to some but annoying or even offensive to others. Surprisingly, he said he never received a negative comment, and the shirts had served well as ice breakers and conversation starters.

I have a bumper sticker on my wall at work that matches the one on my truck that says "Elect Jesus Your Life Leader"[43] In my mind, the main benefit of *billboards* like these is that they keep the name of Jesus on the forefront of your coworkers' minds. Even if they don't by themselves lead someone to Christ or even to a conversation with you about Christ, they may be planting a seed that will eventually bear fruit.

There will always be those who judge you to be self-righteous because you have a *Christian billboard*. You can't control what others think. You *can* control what *you* think, so make sure you're *not* being self-righteous. At the same time, don't let what others say or think stop you from sharing the good news.

Making Disciples vs. Sharing the Gospel

I've heard it taught that the Great Commission in Matthew 28 doesn't actually tell us to share the Gospel or to lead others to salvation, but rather it tells us to make disciples[44].

You might say this is splitting hairs, but I think it's an important distinction. Although sharing the Gospel and leading others to salvation is important, we as individuals and as churches often forget about the importance of discipleship.

The fact that Jesus used the term "disciples" in Matthew 28:19 is an indication of just how important this is. This doesn't mean we don't need to share the Gospel, but it shouldn't stop there. Making disciples is much more than just telling someone about Jesus dying on the cross and helping them to be born again. It's about teaching others and helping them to mature spiritually and to be a fully committed follower of Christ.

> Then Jesus said to those Jews who believed Him, "If you abide in My word, you are My disciples indeed. And you shall know the truth, and the truth shall make you free."
>
> John 8:31–32 (NKJV)

In this passage, Jesus tells us what it takes to be a disciple (abiding in His Word). It makes sense, then, that in order to make disciples, we need to share His Word.

Create Sanctuaries

> Let us think of ways to motivate one another
> to acts of love and good works. And let us not
> neglect our meeting together, as some people do,
> but encourage one another, especially now that
> the day of his return is drawing near.
>
> Hebrews 10:24-25 (NLT)

These verses are often quoted to encourage believers to consistently attend their local churches. Another great application of this verse, in my opinion, is to bring believers together outside of the four walls of the church. After all, the church is really just a collection of believers, not a bunch of buildings. I've heard it said that the early Christian church members met together in their homes.

In churches we've been a part of in the past, my wife and I have participated in *home groups* where members who live close to each other get together in someone's home, usually once a week, to break bread, socialize, go through some teaching, and in various ways share with each other our Christian walk or journey. Though not necessary, usually there is some common bond within a home group, in addition to our church affiliation and where we live, that allows us to relate to each other, help each other, and grow together more effectively. This common bond can be family status, age, gender, or some other factor.

I've been able to grow in my faith by participating in and being a part of a variety of what I call *sanctuaries for men*. In these groups, Christian men are able to open up about issues that affect men in particular, while at the same time be a mutual source of support and encouragement to each other. We talk about our roles as husbands and fathers at home as well as our various roles at work and in the marketplace. We also discuss the unique temptations and challenges that we face in all of our roles. These have been big, formal events as with Promise Keepers[45] as well as smaller groups, including Saturday morning breakfasts.

Similarly, my wife has participated in a number of Bible studies designed specifically for women, often based on a study from Beth Moore[46]. Through these studies, my wife has developed some great friendships, grown in her faith and knowledge of Scripture, and experienced an increase in her enthusiasm and passion for God.

Before we moved to our current location, I was participating briefly with a group of men who were committed to meeting once a week for three years, based on the time Jesus spent with His disciples, at which time they planned to each form their own group. It's been over three years since we moved, and I'm happy to report that they stuck with their commitment and faithfully met for three years and have now split up to form their own groups.

Through these events and groups, I've built friendships—real, substantial, and lasting friendships— unlike any I've ever had. I've also maintained and increased my energy and passion for God and my Christian walk.

What, you may ask, does this have to do with work? Well, I've also developed sanctuaries at my workplace.

Making Adjustments

My first attempt at creating a sanctuary at work was not very fruitful, as I described in the beginning of this chapter.

Why didn't that Bible study at Burger King work out? I don't know for sure, but later after I lost my job there and started in a new job, I tried to learn from my experience. In my new job, when I wanted to start a group Bible study, I didn't send out any mass e-mails to coworkers or post a sign on the bulletin board, but instead invited other believers through one-on-one conversations.

I asked my HR manager if it was okay for me to hold a Bible study in one of the conference rooms at work during lunch. I also decided to ask him for permission whenever I would post anything on the bulletin board of a spiritual nature, like posting a flyer announcing a men's breakfast at church. He's always said yes to my requests.

Since I started the weekly lunch group, it has grown slowly to as many as five, though there are times when no one shows up. When we do meet, it's been a blessing for me and I believe for everyone else involved. For me, it's great to have a time when I can be free to share my faith openly with others at work in a safe environment without worrying about offending anyone.

Another very meaningful sanctuary for me has been one where I meet with a friend at work once every one or two weeks one-on-one. We grab a conference room over lunch, watch a video teaching from a teacher we like, and share with each other our thoughts on the teaching. It's also a chance for us to share what's going on in our lives, get advice about important decisions we're facing at work and at home, and to pray for each other and get advice about important decisions we're facing at work and at home.

What They Are and What They Are Not

"Honor all *people*. Love the brotherhood. Fear God. Honor the king." (1 Peter 2:17 NKJV).

That verse says a number of things to me, including a command to love other believers. Combining that verse with the command to gather together as believers (Hebrews 10:25), leads me to seek ways to join with other believers whenever I can.

I've come to realize what these sanctuaries I've been involved in at work *are* and what they are *not*, or rather what they *should be* and what they should *not be*.

- **A Source of Encouragement**–They *are* a place where we as believers can encourage each other, pray for each other, and seek and receive support for what's going on in our lives, both at work and at home.
- **A Place to Disciple and Be Discipled**–They have the potential to be a place where we can grow as disciples as we counsel and advise each other.
- **Evangelism Launching Pad**–These sanctuaries make us better equipped to reach out to nonbelievers and others at work and to stay more focused on God throughout the day.

JESUS IS AT WORK

One thing these sanctuaries are *not* is they're *not* (or at least shouldn't be) a place to talk about others at work. We made a rule early on in our weekly group that we would not allow our group to become a gossip session in any way. Preferably, we would never speak about anyone else we work with, but if we did in order to share one of our experiences, then we were not allowed to use any names.

Another thing these sanctuaries are *not* is they're *not* a place to evangelize to others within the group, since the participants are already believers.

Don't Build a Bubble

As great as sanctuaries are, there's a danger of focusing so much on them in your life and at your work that you create a Christian bubble and completely insulate yourselves from nonbelievers and others with whom you don't have much in common.

Don't forget the model that Jesus provided for us. He created sanctuaries in His life and poured into His disciples, particularly His inner circle of Peter, James, and John.

At the same time, Jesus was a consistent friend to sinners. Unlike the pharisees of His time, He didn't judge the prostitutes, drunks, and tax collectors but instead spent time with them, including going into their homes, and He loved on them. He didn't condone their sin (John 8:11), but He didn't condemn their sin either. He loved them unconditionally just as He loves you and me.

We shouldn't be blending in with unbelievers at work, nor should we be snubbing our noses at them.

As I heard one preacher Alistair Begg put it:

> God's people are in danger of two extremes, one being absorbed by the culture, thereby having people to talk to and nothing to say, or being isolated from the culture, having something to say and no one to talk to[47].

I'm Not So Sure About All This...

You may be resistant to taking my advice and living out these *general* divine assignments described in the final section of this book. This may be well outside of your comfort zone. It's always difficult to break out of your routine and try something different, no matter what the setting, but even more so at your work where most of us have settled into a fairly comfortable, predictable routine.

You may be concerned about making some people at your work uncomfortable or that you'll be offending them or somehow infringing on their rights. Perhaps this is all in conflict with some of the creeds by which you live your life, including some common ones like "you don't talk about religion and politics" or "my faith is a private matter."

You may be wondering what your boss or the HR manager might think; specifically, you may be worrying that you'll lose your job or limit your ability to be promoted.

I probably don't have all the answers to these questions, but consider the following:

Remember Your Purpose

If these issues are a big deal for you, you may be putting the cart before the horse, so to speak. You may be trying to live out your assignment without being firmly planted in your purpose—to love God.

There's a reason why I placed "Act Like Jesus" at the end of the book. I believe that if you focus on loving God as the purpose of your work *first*, your desire will naturally be to act like Jesus, including in the ways described in the last part of this book. If, instead, you start out by just trying to fill out a checklist of dos and don'ts, you're likely to fail. That's legalism. That's climbing a ladder without looking to see where you placed the ladder. That's being a Pharisee.

Once you're clear on what the divine purpose is for your work and start living it out, your priorities will be different. You'll be more eternally- and spiritually-minded. What other people think and what *natural* consequences might occur as a result of actions you take will not take on the same level of importance if you know that you are living within your divine purpose.

Start your focus in the right place—on seeking God, and not on the activities that will otherwise naturally come from having a divine purpose at your work. If you do that, these divine assignments at your work will seem less like a burden or obligation and more like an exciting opportunity to live out your divine purpose.

Don't Be a Thief

You should respect the fact that you're being paid by your employer for something, primarily your time and what you do with your time while you're on the job. If you're using your time for something other than what you've been hired for, you're stealing from your employer, just the same as if you took home paperclips from the office supply cabinet.

Your conscience, the Holy Spirit, should guide you in this area, but you may want to think of what your comfort level is regarding how much of your time you spend talking about non-work-related items while you're at work. Whatever standard you have for how much time you spend talking about your family, what you're doing over the weekend, your personal hobbies, etc., should probably be the standard you hold for yourself when it comes to discussing your faith.

Another way of thinking of this is that you and everyone else at work are going to spend some of their time while on the job talking about personal matters; it's just a question of what you use your personal talk time to discuss. Will it be the latest *American Idol* episode or something that will actually build up someone spiritually?

You May Lose Your Job

Let's be honest. There is no guarantee that you will not pay some kind of price in natural terms by living out your divine purpose at work with a divine assignment, in particular sharing the good news and creating sanctuaries. Remember that the Bible tells us that not everyone will want to hear the truth when we share it or see it when we live it out.

"Do not marvel, my brethren, if the world hates you." (1 John 3:13 NKJV).

The goal of this book is certainly not for you to lose your job. Having said that, although the Bible says that God will honor those who are humble and obedient to

Him (James 4:6, 1 Peter 5:5), your reward may come from somewhere other than earthly promotion at your job, and it's possible you may even lose your job, depending on how you handle yourself, how open the culture at your work is to Jesus, as well as what attacks you receive from Satan in the process.

Remember that God loves you and wants what is best for you. If you're truly seeking God and being obedient in your actions to what He speaks to you through the Bible and to your heart, how can you go wrong? If what is best for you is to find success in your current job by promotions or other forms of earthly favor, then that is exactly what will happen. If what is best for you is to lose your job so God can open a better door for you, one more in line with His plan for you, then that is exactly what will happen.

Either way, God has a better plan for you than you could ever dream up for yourself, so trust Him with that superior plan.

When I lost my job in 2009, I was told my position was eliminated due to budget cuts and not due to any performance issue. Was it partially or even primarily because I was living out the divine assignments we've been discussing? There's no way for me to know for sure. What I do know is this:

1. Within two months of losing my job, God provided a better job (more interesting work, more pay, in a better working environment, a better boss, greater potential for advancement), in a better area of the country (better climate, more beautiful scenery, more things to do), with a better

house for the same cost as our old one (brand new, almost twice the square footage, larger lot with woods, and a bigger yard that allowed us to have a dog; too many other great things to mention), and in a new church that helped us to grow spiritually in new ways.

2. Through me, God sowed spiritual seeds with coworkers at my old job that I believe will grow into spiritual fruit for years, perhaps lifetimes and generations to come.

3. I had a sense of divine purpose at my job long before I lost my job and continue to do so at my new job.

If you are obedient and you seek God, He will be faithful and you will reap the rewards of the seeds that are sown.

Think Eternally

I also encourage you to look at this issue from an eternal perspective. "Set your mind on things above, not on things on the earth." (Colossians 3:2 NKJV).

> Do not lay up for yourselves treasures on earth, where moth and rust destroy and where thieves break in and steal; but lay up for yourselves treasures in heaven, where neither moth nor rust destroys and where thieves do not break in and steal.
>
> Matthew 6:19–20 NKJV

I don't think that on our deathbeds we'll be regretting living out our divine assignments at our work.

I'd like to think that the people God touches through my actions at work will share with me in heaven how their lives were impacted, and we'll all be able to celebrate these *treasures* for all time.

Practical Advice on Acting Like Jesus

For my final thought on how best to *act like Jesus* at your work, I'd like to share some practical advice on this topic I found online (from Pastor Melvin Newland)[48]:

1. First of all, don't brag. Don't go to work & brag about how wonderful your Christian life is. Don't brag about how righteous you are & how much sin you have overcome, & how you used to drink & carouse & be unfaithful, but now you are a model husband or wife & you don't drink anymore. Don't brag. That will only turn them off.

   Self-righteousness has always been repulsive. It simply won't work. Don't brag.

2. Don't nag. Don't carry a big Bible under your arm, & every time somebody cusses pull it out & say, "Look here. It says, 'Thou shalt not swear.'" Every time they brag about what a hangover they have, don't pull it out & say, "Look, it says, 'All drunkards are going to hell.'" Don't do that.

   Because all you're going to do is turn them away. You may think that you are being bold. No, you're not being bold. You're simply turning them away.

3. So don't brag, & don't nag, & don't lag. As a Christian it is important for you to do your work & do it well, to set an example for others, to be there on time, maybe even early, to do your job & maybe a little bit of their job if they're falling behind, to help them out in any way you possibly can.

If you're lazy, if you're slothful on the job, then that's a poor testimony for the Lord. So do your job & do it well, as if you are doing it for Christ.

4. Don't sag. Be really careful not to go back to your old way of life. Be really careful not to listen to their language & start to use it yourself. Be really careful not to see the bright lights of a far country & be enticed. Make sure you keep your eyes fixed on Jesus.

Then, if you keep your eyes fixed on Jesus, if you don't use their language, if you react in a different way to problems & difficulties that come, sooner or later they will come up & say, "I notice you're different. What has caused the difference?"

They will, because inside they're hurting. Inside they're looking for answers & solutions. And if you can mirror what Christ can do in a life, sooner or later the door will swing open for you to share gently & tenderly your testimony with them. If you'll just be there every day, setting that solid consistent Christian example.

Epilogue

Be a First-Chair Christian and Let That Fire Burn

Are you *all-in*?
I hope your reading of this book has left you feeling encouraged and motivated to seek out and live out God's purpose as well as His assignment for you at your work.

I hope you're excited by the prospect that you don't have to settle for what the world has told you to expect from your work and your career.

Just as with anything in your Christian walk, there will be days and times when you question if this is real. There will be times when you wonder whether God really cares about your work.

Satan will join you in this pity party on those days and will probably actually host the party. He'll plant seeds of doubt in your head, asking you to consider whether your work is truly worthy of being considered *divine*, or whether it is, after all, just a way to pay the bills, get by, and hold on until retirement.

When these doubts rise up or you're feeling beaten down after a bad day at work, I challenge you to ask yourself if you've truly committed to being all-in as a Christian, including every aspect of your life.

If the honest answer is that no, you haven't gone all-in, or you're not sure, then read on…

Become a First-Chair Christian

One thing I've found has helped me have a divine purpose and assignment about my work on a consistent basis (even on those bad days) is to commit to fully integrate Jesus Christ and my relationship with Him into every aspect of my life, to be consistent in the sense that I'm the same person spiritually at home, at work, at church, and with friends.

One of my favorite sermons that really helped shape my thinking in this area came from our pastor at the time, Cam Huxford, and it was about the three Christian chairs. I'll paraphrase it here[49].

> You could say that there are three kinds of Christians, first-chair Christians, second-chair Christians, and third-chair Christians.
>
> First-chair Christians are those who fully integrate their faith into every aspect of their lives. They are the same person at work that they are at home and at church.
>
> They don't feel embarrassed to talk about their faith at work because that's who they are. They don't have to worry about catching themselves swearing at church because swearing is not

practiced in other parts of their lives and is simply not a part of who they are.

They don't have to worry if someone from their church works at the same place they do because they don't act differently at work than they do at church.

Their life is less like a roller coaster and more like a smooth ride through the countryside.

They're confident where they'll be spending eternity but are focused on the *now* and on living out their faith and God's purpose for every aspect of their lives.

Second-chair Christians compartmentalize their lives.

They go to church on Sunday. They try to be good people and think of themselves as better than most.

They consider themselves to be Christian and identify themselves to others as Christians, but the extent to which their actions and their behaviors are Christ-like vary significantly from one facet of their life to the next.

They act one way at church on Sunday, another way on the golf course with their buddies. They act one way around their family and another way at the cafeteria table at work during break.

They find themselves spending much of their time putting on a show for others, constantly gauging who they're talking with and adjusting their behavior and the content of their conversation as their audience changes.

They may or may not have heaven as their eternal destination, but they believe they're going to heaven. They think of their Christianity more as an insurance policy.

They fit their religion into their lives but are careful not to let it upset or interfere too greatly with all the priorities they're juggling.

Third-chair Christians don't even try to fit their Christianity into their lives, though they may call themselves Christians.

They may occasionally go to church, but otherwise don't let God get in the way of their life. Their secular worldview is fully integrated into their lives.

Though they may be considered *nice people* by others they know, there's no evidence by their behavior nor their lifestyle that they are Christian. They live for today and they live more or less for themselves.

They tend to think of life as a bunch of gray areas rather than as black and white or right and wrong, and they find peace in being open-minded and tolerant of a number of different worldviews.

They're most likely not going to heaven, but they're not worried about it because they don't think anyone really knows what's true or not, and so they aren't too concerned about whether or not they get it right.

Ironically, the only one of the three who does *not* have peace is the second-chair Christian.

First-chair Christians have peace because their faith is fully integrated into their lives.

Third-chair Christians have peace (though a false peace) because their secular worldview is fully integrated into their lives.

Second-chair Christians have one foot in both worlds, and have the most anxiety because they're trying to have it both ways. Their life is not integrated and as a result it's confusing and frustrating.

First-chair Christians are more likely to face persecution and attacks from the devil, but they have all the support they'll ever need to face those trials from their Father in heaven.

Second-chair Christians tend to seek God when they're in a bind but make the mistake of thinking they can pretty much handle life on their own when things seem to be going well.

This sermon had a huge impact on me and led me to three immediate conclusions: First, I knew that what he said was true. Second, I recognized myself as being a second-chair Christian. Third, I knew that I wanted to be a first-chair Christian.

I'm on a never-ending spiritual journey just as we all are, and I've no more earned salvation than anyone else, but I'm happy to say that I am today a first-chair Christian and I highly recommend it to everyone.

As a first-chair Christian, am I *better* than any other Christian? The answer is no, not in my own strength. I am, however, better equipped to face life and all its trials. I am better able to overcome doubt and frustration in my walk with God. And I'm in a much better position to have a divine purpose and assignment for my work.

Peaceful Divine Frustration

To be honest, even though the concept of the three Christian chairs was helpful to me in many ways, during my most frustrating days its explanation didn't feel quite right.

There have been times when I have seen second-chair Christians in my life that seem to have it all together and to be very happy. At times, they seem to have the best of both worlds, while I'm feeling disappointed with myself and my own spiritual walk, and I've wondered why.

It shouldn't work that way, I've thought. *It's the double-minded person, the person who's not completely committed to the Lord, who should be frustrated, right? I should be consistently experiencing victory, joy, peace and the other blessings God has promised me, right?*

I heard a teaching that helped me with this frustration and gave me a better perspective[50].

This teaching showed me that in some ways, those Christians who don't expect anything supernatural, or *divine*, in their lives but rather are basically waiting for heaven in the afterlife (what I might call second-chair Christians), can have a less frustrating life experience at times as a result of them having lower expectations than those that are expecting the supernatural in their everyday life (what I might call first-chair Christians).

Frustration can sometimes be what we feel as first-chair Christians, but we should not let that get us down, and we should not assume that lacking certain frustrations is the same as having divine peace and joy.

Having frustration just because bad things happen or because we have a bad attitude is one thing. Another thing entirely is frustration that comes from wanting to be closer to God and having high expectations for the supernatural presence of God seeming real in our lives. That second kind of frustration will bring us closer to God and strengthen our faith.

Through that *divine frustration,* we can have the peace that transcends all understanding no matter what we're *feeling*.

Be Consumed

Bottom line is, don't let the kind of frustration I'm describing, especially if you're experiencing it at your work, keep you from being a first-chair Christian and on fire for God.

In Revelation, the angel of the Lord instructs John to write to the church in Laodicea, "I know your deeds, that you are neither cold nor hot; I wish that you were cold or hot.

So because you are lukewarm, and neither hot nor cold, I will spit you out of My mouth." (Revelation 3:15–16 NKJV)

The Bible says that God is a "consuming fire." (Deuteronomy 4:24 NKJV).

For me, being a first-chair Christian is about letting God *consume* you, allowing you to be hot and not lukewarm. It's about making and keeping a commitment to submit to Jesus Christ as Lord and Savior of your work, your family, your finances, your hobbies, your talents… your life, even when you're tested and frustrated.

As you finish this book and contemplate your next step, I encourage you to seek God in your workplace and experience your divine purpose and assignment there by beginning with the first step of choosing to be a first-chair Christian.

Let God's consuming fire inside you burn while you're at work for the rest of your life on earth and forever more.

Appendix:
Discussion Questions

To be used by the individual reader or as part of a group study.

Part 1: Here's The Problem

Chapter 1: First Things First

1. Are you born again?
2. If not or you're not sure, do you agree that you must be born again to go to heaven?
3. What do think you have to do in order to be born again?
4. If you've never done this, will you, right now, say a prayer and receive the free gift of salvation and make Jesus your Savior and your Lord? For the benefit of others who are with you, would you say a prayer even if you already know you're born again?
5. Is there one person in your life you can think of right now that needs to be born again?

Chapter 2: Apathy and Misery in the Workplace

1. According to some surveys, 65 percent of Americans are unhappy with their jobs and go to work simply because they have no other choice. Do you count yourself among those 65 percent?
2. Can you relate to ever having felt like Sam and wondered if there was something more than the work that you do?
3. Can you think of phrases that you hear your coworkers say that indicate they are lacking in joy and purpose when it comes to their job?
4. Have you ever put on a happy face at work, trying to show your coworkers that everything is okay when in reality it wasn't?

Chapter 3: Out of the Frying Pan...

1. Do you ever compare yourself to your pastor or someone doing *full-time* ministry and wonder if your work is as important as theirs?
2. Have you ever taken on volunteer commitments, as Kevin did, primarily trying to make up for a lack of purpose you were feeling about your work?
3. Can you think of some nonnegotiable commitments in your life that you know God wants for you to keep?
4. Do you agree that having a good attitude toward your job should be among your list of nonnegotiable commitments?
5. Do you agree that hobbies have the potential to be unhealthy and misguided? If so, can you describe an example of this?

Part 2: Dream with Purpose

Chapter 4: Start with Your Purpose

1. Have you had "God moments," like the one described at the men's breakfast, where God spoke to you through someone else? Describe one or two and how you allowed them to impact your life.

2. As a believer and therefore the bride of Jesus, do you agree that we don't have to perform for Him to get Him to love us?

3. Share your experience going through the 1 Corinthians exercise. Did this shed some light on your current attitude toward your work and how important it is to love God above anything else you might *do*?

4. Do you agree that when it comes to loving God, our focus should be on His love for us rather than our love for Him?

5. What do you think about some of the suggestions for loving God while at work, including prayer and praise as well as meditating on God's Word? Do you do those now? If not, can you picture yourself doing these in the future?

6. Do you agree that you'll have more wisdom and peace as a result of loving God while you're at work? How would that affect other parts of your life?

Chapter 5: Next, Find Your Assignment

1. Have you ever taken an aptitude test? What were the results of taking that test?

2. Do you agree that the world (conventional wisdom) recommends that you primarily consider your personality, strengths, desire, and experience when picking your perfect job or career?

3. 1 Thessalonians says "Now may the God of peace Himself sanctify you completely; and may your whole spirit, soul, and body be preserved blameless at the coming of our Lord Jesus Christ." (1 Thessalonians 5:23 NKJV). Do you believe your identity is defined by your spirit and not by your body and soul (mind, will, and emotions)? Put another way, do you agree that you *are* a spirit, you *have* a soul, and you *live* in a body?

4. Have you ever pursued your dreams, including your work and career goals, based primarily on your desires, while at the same time not pursued and loved God with all your heart? What was the end result?

5. Read through again the action plan at the end of the chapter, including the Bible verses mentioned. Do you think this kind of plan could work for you?

Chapter 6: Let God Be Your Promoter

1. Have you experienced a time when you believe God wanted you to stay in a situation even though it didn't feel right to *you*?

2. If you answered yes, looking back, do you think any of the four possible reasons listed why God might have wanted you to stay make sense to you now?

3. "Your word is a lamp to my feet and a light to my path." (Psalm 119:105 NKJV). Can you think of a time when you were not in God's Word and as a result either stepped off the path of your job or career or stood stuck in one place in that path?

4. Read the story of Joseph in Genesis 37–45. How can you apply how Joseph handled his circumstances to your career?

5. Do you agree that you can get a "rhema" or personal Word from God about your career by first focusing on His "logos" by reading and meditating on the Bible?

Part 3: Think Like Jesus

Chapter 7: What Jesus Thinks about Work

1. Genesis 2:2, Malachi 3:6, and John 1:1 show that God has always been a worker and always will be. Since you're made in God's image, does it make sense to you that you were made to work (in a good way)?

2. God referred to His work as "good" repeatedly when He created the universe. How often do you say the same thing about the work you do?

3. The story of Adam and Eve shows that God originally intended for work to be good. The author gives three reasons to support the idea that our work today is still good. Do any or all of these make sense to you?

4. Glance through all the Scripture verses showing the benefits of work. How many of those have you found to be true in your life?

5. Do you think of God as your primary boss? If you don't, how do you think your attitude toward your work would change if you did?

Chapter 8: What Jesus Thinks about Money

1. Read Malachi 8:3-11. Do think the command given by God to tithe applies to you? If you said yes, are you being obedient to that command?

2. Read Proverbs 22:7. Is there any person or institution to whom you are currently a servant because of a debt that you owe? If so, do you plan to change that? If so, how?

3. Using the definition of a "good steward" as someone who values highly and makes the most of what they are asked to be responsible for, of what things in your life are you a "good steward"? Of what things could you be a better steward?

4. Why do you think the Bible cautions us so many times not to *love* money?

5. Psalm 35:27 says that God "has pleasure in the prosperity of His servant." (Psalm 35:27 NKJV). Do you believe that God is happy when you prosper financially?

6. Jesus said "But seek first the kingdom of God and His righteousness, and all these things shall be added to you." (Matthew 6:33 NKJV). To what *things* do you think He was referring?

Chapter 9: You're Already a Missionary

1. Do you think it's correct to say that full-time ministry only applies to clergymen, pastors, foreign missionaries, and those preaching or ministering God's Word through TV, books, music, and the like? Why or why not?
2. Jesus didn't tell Zaccheus to quit his job but He did ask Matthew to do so, even though they were both tax collectors. What does this tell you?
3. Have you ever been in a situation, like the person on the plane, where you changed how you acted after you found out the person you were talking with was a pastor? How did you change?
4. If you were to guess, over the course of your working career, how many people do you think you know and influence through your job who will never meet your pastor (please specify a number)? Does knowing that change your attitude about the importance of your job in Kingdom terms?
5. Have you ever felt guilty that you weren't in what most people would consider to be full-time ministry? Do you think God wanted you to feel guilty?

Chapter 10: Think Differently about Retirement

1. In the passage from Larry Burkett's book, it says that there is only one direct reference to retirement in the Bible, relating specifically to the Levites in the Old Testament. Does this surprise you? What does this say to you?

2. In general, what do you think about what Larry Burkett says in the passage quoted about retirement?

3. Do you agree with the statement "When it comes to prosperity, too many people in America, including some Christians, are too focused on their own personal prosperity and not on *posterity*, namely the prosperity of future generations"? How do you think we should apply this to the issue of saving for the future?

4. During our "working years", do you think it's a mistake to be too focused on our retirement? Why or why not? Can this impact our attitude toward our work?

5. Do you think of your retirement as a finish line or a commencement, namely a transition to another phase in life? How do you envision spending your time after you retire?

Part 4: Act Like Jesus

Chapter 11: Be Great at What You Do

1. Do you believe that in addition to having an opinion on what type of work we should do (a personal work assignment), God also has general work assignments for us, or more specifically, that God has specific *ways* in which He wants us to do our work regardless of our job title?

2. Do you think there are some types of work for which you cannot be pleasing to God, no matter how you conduct yourself in your work?

3. Would your coworkers consider your skills to be more from natural ability or from hard work?

4. Does the performance-oriented culture of America make it easy to give ourselves credit for both our abilities and our hard work instead of giving credit to God?

5. Do you "Work with enthusiasm, as though you were working for the Lord rather than for people." (Ephesians 6: 7 New Living Translation)?

Chapter 12: Model Integrity

1. Do you think honesty is a black-and-white integrity issue, or are there some lies that are acceptable under certain circumstances?

2. Does the company you work for have rules of ethics regarding preferential treatment, or more specifically giving and receiving of gifts? If you're not sure, do you know where to find them? Do they line up with Deuteronomy 16:19 and Matthew 22:16?

3. Do you give your coworkers the same respect and professional courtesy even if you don't like them too much?

4. When hearing gossip or foul language at work, do you typically respond with any or all of the three levels described (not participating, walking away, and confronting), or do you join in and participate?

Chapter 13: Love and Serve Others

1. Can you think of a time when you loved or served a coworker? What was the result?

2. Do you think it's significant that the first four of the Ten Commandments deal with our relationship with God, while the other six deal with our relationship with other people? If yes, explain why.

3. When you've asked someone else the question "how are you doing" in the hallway at work, has anyone ever said something that made you think something wasn't quite right? How did you respond?

4. Have you ever prayed with someone while you're at work? If not, why haven't you? Do you plan to do so in the future?

5. Do you consider yourself to be a servant leader?

Chapter 14: Share the Good News and Make Disciples

1. Have you ever tried to share the Gospel or create disciples and been frustrated or disappointed as the author was in the Burger King story?

2. Do you think the atheist was justified in his anger toward Christians who don't evangelize?

3. Have you ever seen someone at your work wearing an "in your face" Jesus kind of T-shirt like the custodian? If you did, what did you think of that? If you haven't, what would you think about that if you did see this at work?

4. Do you think that, as Christians, we focus too much on sharing the Gospel and not enough on making disciples?

5. Are you worried about losing your job or offending someone if you "act like Jesus" at your work as described in this last section of the book?

Epilogue

1. Are you a first-, second-, or third-chair Christian?
2. Why are second-chair Christians the only one of the three types described that don't have peace?
3. Can you think of examples of first-, second-, and third-chair Christians in your life?
4. Is it possible to find peace while experiencing a divine frustration that comes from persistently seeking the supernatural presence of God in your life?
5. Are you lukewarm, hot, or cold when it comes to your walk with God? Explain.

Endnotes

1. Kelly, Walt. "www.thisdayinquotes.com." Last modified APRIL 22, 2013. Accessed October 5, 2013. http://www.thisdayinquotes.com/search?q=we have met the enemy and he is us.

2. Billy Graham Evangelistic Association, "BillyGraham.org." Accessed October 6, 2013. http://peacewithgod.jesus.net/but-have-eternal-life/.

3. Newland, Melvin. Ridge Chapel, "Sermon Central." Last modified September 1991. Accessed October 5, 2013. http://www.sermoncentral.com/sermons/labor-day—taking-christ-with-you-melvin-newland-sermon-on-holidays-civic-32931.asp?Page=1.

4. Dave Tomlinson, "How Many Hours Will You Work In Your Lifetime?," *ArticlesBase* (blog), February 9, 2010, http://www.articlesbase.com/advice-articles/how-many-hours-will-you-work-in-your-lifetime-1841025.html.

5. Based on The Random House Dictionary, "Dictionary.com." Accessed October 5, 2013. http://dictionary.reference.com/browse/apathy?s=t.

6. Michael Trogdon, (Bishop for Kingdom Life Community Church, Asheboro, NC), Message given at Community Men's Breakfast, Central United Methodist Church,

Asheboro, NC, sponsored by Randolph Christian Men's Ministry "Our Purpose," July 23, 2011.

7. Wommack, Andrew, "Effortless Change," Web, http://wwww.awmi.net/extra/audio/1018.

8. Andrew Wommack, *A Better Way to Pray*, (Tulsa, Oklahoma : Harrison House Publishers, 2007).

9. "An Officer and a Gentleman." Paramount Pictures July 28 1982.

10. Bill Godwin, *The Power of a Dream (God's Dreams for You)*, (Blue Rocket LLC, 2001).

11. Jon Acuff, *Quitter: Closing the Gap Between Your Day Job & Your Dream Job*, (Brentwood, TN: Lampo Press, 2011).

12. Wommack, Andrew, "Spirit, Soul & Body," Web, http://www.awmi.net/extra/audio/1027.

13. Wommack, Andrew, "How To Follow God's Will," Web, http://www.awmi.net/extra/audio/1067.

14. Ramsey, Dave, "Financial Peace University," DVD.

15. Shirley, Delron, "Charis Bible College Campus Days," Web, http://www.awmi.net/extra/conference_videos/campus10/wednesday.

16. *The Hebrew-Greek Key Word Study Bible, King James Version*, (Chattanooga, TN: AMG International, Inc, 2008), 2180-2181, 2236.

17. Sowing Circle, "blueletterbible.org." Accessed October 5, 2013. http://www.blueletterbible.org/search/search.cfm?Criteria=work&t=NKJV

18. Sowing Circle, "blueletterbible.org." Accessed October 5, 2013. http://www.blueletterbible.org/search/search.cfm?Criteria=labor&t=NKJV

19. Dave Ramsey, *Financial Peace Revisited*, (Viking Adult, 2002).

20. Ramsey, Dave, "Financial Peace University," DVD

21. Garner, Deborah. "Faith For Finances" Recorded June 3 2012. Victory Fellowship Church. compact disc

22. Based on The Random House Dictionary, "Dictionary. com." Accessed October 5, 2013. http://dictionary. reference.com/browse/steward?s=t.

23. James Strong, *Strong*, (Iowa Falls, IA: World Bible Publishers, 1991), Concordance 1099, Greek Dictionary of The New Testament 81.

24. Merriam-Webster, "merriam-webster.com." Accessed October 5, 2013. http://www.merriam-webster.com/ dictionary/disciple.

25. *The Hebrew-Greek Key Word Study Bible, King James Version*, (Chattanooga, TN: AMG International, Inc, 2008), 2076.

26. Garner, Deborah. "Faith For Finances" Recorded June 3 2012. Victory Fellowship Church. compact disc

27. Garner, Deborah. "Faith For Finances" Recorded June 3 2012. Victory Fellowship Church. compact disc

28. Chad Brand, Charles Draper, and Archie England, *Holman Illustrated Bible Dictionary*, (Nashville, TN: Holman Bible Publishers, 2003), 1349.

29. Dave Stewart, (Missions Pastor, Savannah Christian Church, Savannah, GA), Message given at Savannah Men of Integrity Breakfast, circa 2006.

30. Griffin Marion, (Retired Medical Surgeon), Comments after reviewing manuscript. September 25, 2013.

31. Larry Burkett, *Preparing for Retirement*, (Moody Press, 1992), 24-31.

32. The American Heritage® Dictionary of the English Language, Fourth Edition copyright ©2000 by Houghton Mifflin Company. Updated in 2009. Published by Houghton Mifflin Company. All rights reserved., "The

Free Dictionary by Farlex." Accessed October 5, 2013. http://www.thefreedictionary.com/finish line.

33. Based on The Random House Dictionary, "Dictionary.com." Accessed October 5, 2013. http://dictionary.reference.com/browse/commencement?s=t.

34. Cam Huxford, (Frequent comment made in sermons), Savannah Christian Church, Savannah, GA 2005-2008.

35. Merriam-Webster, "merriam-webster.com." Accessed October 5, 2013. http://www.merriam-webster.com/dictionary/integrity.

36. Arroyo Ed, (Sermon), Central Carolina Community Church, Asheboro, NC. 2012

37. About.com, "About.com Quotations." Accessed October 5, 2013. http://quotations.about.com/od/stillmorefamous people/a/RalphWaldoEmer8.htm.

38. Andrew Wommack, *A Better Way to Pray*, (Tulsa, Oklahoma: Harrison House Publishers, 2007).

39. Matt Rollins, (Fellow Christian), Conversation while test driving a pick-up truck. June 5, 2012.

40. Franz, James. Way of the Master, a ministry of Living Waters Publications, "WayoftheMaster.com." Accessed October 5, 2013. http://wayofthemaster.com/atheistletter.shtml.

41. Tackett, Del. "Tour One." *The Truth Project*. Focus on the Family. DVD

42. Way of the Master, a ministry of Living Waters Publications, "WayoftheMaster.com." Accessed October 5, 2013. http://wayofthemaster.com/index.shtml.

43. "ElectJesus.net." Accessed October 5, 2013. http://electjesus.net/.

44. Wommack, Andrew, *Summer Family Bible Conference 2010*, Web, http://www.awmi.net/extra/conference_videos/sfbc10/

tuesdaytp://www.awmi.net/extra/conference_videos/sfbc10/monday.

45. Promise Keepers, "Promise Keepers." Accessed October 5, 2013. http://www.promisekeepers.org/.

46. Moore, Beth. Living Proof Ministries, "Living Proof with Beth Moore." Accessed October 5, 2013. http://www.lproof.org/.

47. Begg, Alistair, "A Christian Manifesto, Part 1," *A Christian Manifesto–A Study in Luke 6*, Web, http://www.truthforlife.org/resources/sermon/a-christian-manifesto-pt1/.

48. Melvin Newland, "Labor Day–Taking Christ With You," *SermonCentral.com* (1991), http://www.sermoncentral.com/sermons/labor-day—taking-christ-with-you-melvin-newland-sermon-on-holidays-civic-32931.asp?page=4 (accessed October 5, 2013).

49. Cam Huxford, (Senior Pastor, Savannah Christian Church), Described in a Sermon "The Three Christian Chairs," 2005.

50. Wommack, Andrew, "Week 37 of 2011," "You've Already Got It", *TV Archives for The Gospel Truth TV Program*, Web, http://www.awmi.net/tv/2011/week37.